DOUGLAS C. MANN

™

HOW ARTISTS CAN
SERVE GOD AND
LOVE THE WORLD

IVP Books

An imprint of InterVarsity Press
Downers Grove, Illinois

InterVarsity Press
P.O. Box 1400, Downers Grove, IL 60515-1426
World Wide Web: www.ivpress.com
Email: email@ivpress.com

©2014 by Douglas C. Mann

InterVarsity Press® is the book-publishing division of InterVarsity Christian Fellowship/USA®, a movement of students and faculty active on campus at hundreds of universities, colleges and schools of nursing in the United States of America, and a member movement of the International Fellowship of Evangelical Students. For information about local and regional activities, write Public Relations Dept., InterVarsity Christian Fellowship/USA, 6400 Schroeder Rd., P.O. Box 7895, Madison, WI 53707-7895, or visit the IVCF website at www.intervarsity.org.

All Scripture quotations, unless otherwise indicated, are taken from the Holy Bible, New International Version®. NIV®. Copyright ©1973, 1978, 1984, 2011 by Biblica, Inc.™ Used by permission. All rights reserved.

While all stories in this book are true, some names and identifying information in this book have been changed to protect the privacy of the individuals involved.

Cover design: Cindy Kiple
Images: Abstract background: © Ekely/iStockphoto; splatter: iStockphoto.com
   The Art of Helping Others logo courtesy of Disciple Design
   Photo courtesy of Nataliya Mann Photography
Interior design: Beth Hagenberg

ISBN 978-0-8308-3750-2 (print)
ISBN 978-0-8308-6467-6 (digital)

Printed in the United States of America ∞

Library of Congress Cataloging-in-Publication Data
Mann, Douglas C., 1957-
  The art of helping others : how artists can serve God and love the world
  / Douglas C. Mann.
    pages cm
  Includes bibliographical references.
  ISBN 978-0-8308-3750-2 (pbk. : alk. paper)
  1. Christianity and the arts. 2. Church work. 3. Helping
behavior—Religious aspects—Christianity. 4. Caring—Religious
aspects—Christianity. I. Title.
  BR115.A8M365 2014
  261.5'7--dc23
                   2013040767

P	22	21	20	19	18	17	16	15	14	13	12	11	10	9	8	7	6	5	4	3	2	1
Y	33	32	31	30	29	28	27	26	25	24	23	22	21	20	19	18	17	16	15	14		

To those who choose to make a difference and

for the one who holds the key that unlocks my heart

CONTENTS

You are worthy, our Lord and God,

to receive glory and honor and power,

for you created all things,

and by your will they existed and were created.

Revelation 4:11 (NRSV)

WHY *THIS* BOOK?

This book was written on scraps of paper while I was living in my 1996 Jeep, and also in airports, planes, trains, restaurants, cafés, flats, hotels and on napkins in London, Eastbourne, Amsterdam, Kiev, Kharkov, Nashville, Dallas, Mobile, Denver, Colorado Springs and most points in between.

As has been said, "I enjoy writing; I hate the paperwork."

This book is intended to speak primarily to Christians interested in pursuing art as a lifestyle of social justice, service and worship. Secondarily, I'm aiming at those Christians who want to live more artistically. As such, it speaks to those pursuing creative occupations and ministry as representatives of justice through God's love. This service of work I call "creative incitement," a restorative act reconciling lives wherever and whenever the spirit leads. These pages cover what constitutes the art of Christ followers. I define Christian art as the gloriously diverse creative acts that inspire and incite and reconnect us to the One who heals in gloriously diverse ways.

This book intends to establish that a Christian artist's "product," therefore, is not mere artwork but their very lives. Their product *is* producing.

And what it produces is *creative incitement*.

For Christians who don't identify as artists, this book will expand their understanding of Christian art but also their boundaries of faith, encouraging them to move beyond the borders that our culture and the church have placed on service and social justice. What we think it should look like often gets in the way of what it could look like. Christians who don't create specific works of art are still artists living out their faith creatively in what they model through their Christian life.

This understanding of art, I hope, will inspire us to allow our community's artists the same respect and appreciation as missionaries serving in dark places. Only together will we come to live and produce faithful lives that incite a desire for transformation.

Part One

AWARENESS

For the minister is called to recognize the sufferings of his time in his own heart and make that recognition the starting point of his service. . . .

Nothing can be written about ministry without a deeper understanding of the ways in which the minister can make his own wounds available as a source of healing.

Henri Nouwen, *The Wounded Healer*

1

THE SOMETHING WORTH LOSING EVERYTHING FOR

A man cannot enter the kingdom of Heaven until he has reached the stage of "not caring two straws about his own status."

C. S. LEWIS,
They Stand Together, ed. Walter Hooper

Would you ever consider serving in full-time mission work?"

The first time I met my future mission field director we were in the back room of a pub filled with cigar smoke and pints of Guinness. It was an Irish pub in Nashville on St. Patrick's Day 1996, and I was fresh off a recording set at my job working with marquee artists: Grammy, Billboard and Dove Award winners. We were there along with several other full-time missionaries to Ireland—some American, others Irish. I expected them to be uptight, legalistic and wearing suits and ties, like on the missionary prayer cards that portray these proper, upstanding

The Comfortable Kingdom

Three church steeples rising against a multicolored blue sky with a kite tangled on two steeples and caught in the wind so it abstractly spells the word *love*. This painting is colorful and whimsical, yet poignant in that no doors to a watching world exist on any of the churches. (Courtesy of DankoArtStudio.com) people who love God and even sinners like me.

To my surprise, as we sat around the long wooden table, people laughing, enjoying one another's company, I felt welcomed into the conversation about their unusual (and, I had to admit, *intriguing*) work. I was scrambling, thinking to myself, *You know, I could work well with these people. They all seem to be independent thinkers . . . but they're Christians! They seem to have freedom in Christ—is that for real?* I kept having to remind myself I was with Christians. Either I was dreaming or I stumbled into the wrong pub room.

But the more we talked, the more I leaned in.

And that was when Gary, the director, asked if I'd ever consider full-time mission work.

I swallowed. Hard. I fell quickly back in my chair and began shifting uncomfortably. "So okay," I began, fidgeting with a coaster. "Here's my take on missions. Two weeks is far too long for me. But I can write you a check right now."

No one spoke. I scanned the table. "Besides, my background is in visual art, music and business. I'm not called to that . . . mission-ministry thing you people do. I mean, I'm not a seminary graduate, a pastor, theologian or even a doctor, which is what you need."

Gary smiled and shook his head. "Actually," he said, "that is exactly what we *don't* need. We need more everyday people like yourself that the average person can relate to." He swigged his pint. "With a willingness and openness to be led by the Holy Spirit to do what he wants."

I don't remember what I said. But we continued talking, and I'm sure I got my jaw back up in place and went back to my comfortable life.

And I didn't say it then, but it sounded like a great job description to me.

Over the following months and through many conversations and much prayer, the mission continued to invite me to join them. Their constant refrain was "Come die with us." Of course I asked if this was meant in a figurative sense, a literal sense or both. My future colleagues just smiled and calmly repeated it.

"Come die with us."

Eventually, I accepted. And life has been a series of progressive steps toward an increasingly strange definition of *vocation* ever since.

THE HEART SHAPES THE ART

For a while, not too long ago, I lived off Dauphin Street in Mobile, Alabama. Most early mornings and evenings I'd hear church bells chiming in the distance, floating through the coastal humidity of the Deep South. With the continual reminder of the call to faith, I'd crawl from my bed, stumble, shuffle and bounce off furniture like a pinball propelled toward my first robust caffeinated mega-mug of motivation.

This recurring morning routine would happen in my one-room studio apartment with no interior walls, whose outer walls crumbled bit by bit while its roof leaked like a bucket whenever it rained hard, because the old brick building, a former factory, was riddled with holes.

And like that roof, my heart will leak whatever I choose to put in it. Yours does too. In fact, all of us are like this.

The wood floors, too, had warped to the degree that my office chair would methodically roll toward the west side of the room as I wrote, and like an old-style manual typewriter, I'd repeatedly push myself back up and east to the center of my keyboard.

Like those wood floors, my life shapes to what pours over it. Yours does too. And in fact, we're all like this.

By design, what we put in is what we'll get out. And I believe there's something about being a working artist that makes us come to know this very well.

A STATE OF THE HEART

In the early days of my music career, I was leaking success—success after success. Even though I was part of elite teams that marketed and sold more than 15 million RIAA certified records, which lined my home and work offices with multiplatinum and gold album plaques, I knew there was something missing. The private jets to concerts, limos and hanging with celebrities would leave me with a sense of wading through shallow water with little under the surface. Over time, success caused my heart to harden. I was closed to any suggestion of intimacy with God, even as the Spirit prompted my heart back to him. I became prideful and self-absorbed.

It is not incidental that I was becoming warped while working in the Christian music industry, where intimacy with God is a stated value. I said all the right things and created an acceptable professional persona, all the while hiding behind a safe, superficial façade. I was like the Wizard of Oz—smoke and mirrors all around, but behind the curtain just a little man.

I believed serving God meant trying hard, forging ahead with every fiber, racking up accomplishments and winning people's approval along the way. In reality, I came later to understand, I was far more concerned about building my own kingdom, ostensibly serving others but mostly serving myself.

God used many of the things I did for his good purpose. But

relying on him and the power of the gospel was a distant fading image in my rearview mirror as I traveled further down the motorway of success. Life was good, or so it seemed. Little did I know how much better things could get on the other side of death.

What I took away from that time was that if we lose sight of our need for the good news of Christ, then like a mismanaged bank account we become badly overdrawn and run the real risk of spiritual bankruptcy. Such was the case for me when my status and reputation mattered more to me than God's view of me.

Since I was invited to die, I've made it my goal to ensure my heart leaks the love of God. I'm an artist who seeks a love willing to die for. I've made it my goal to let my life be shaped by that kind of love—going where that divine love takes me, doing what that divine love compels me to do. Because I remember love wasn't always what leaked from my heart and shaped my life.

THE UNRECOGNIZABLE VOICE

I was attending a Christian music summit in Nashville. A guest speaker was teaching on how to discern the will of God in our lives—both professionally and personally. With each talking point came a slight, uncomfortable nudge to my heart. Then came the tipping point: "You know," the speaker said, "if my wife were to call me on the phone, she wouldn't need to identify herself. We talk every day, and I recognize her voice." A pause— it seemed almost infinite—and then, "If God called me on the phone, how would I recognize his voice if I hadn't spent time with him every day? He would practically be a stranger to me; how then could I know his will for me?"

Everything I had been suppressing rose to the surface. I leaned forward and began to weep.

While I was working as an executive in the music industry, nobody around me knew that for almost a year I had refused to pray. I had sensed that God was calling me from my career—a career I worked so hard to achieve—into the foreign territory of ministry. When I did occasionally pray during that time, I dismissed the notion to kneel. I had no interest in answering God's call, and I had spent a year making God no longer my Lord, no longer my friend, but rather a stranger.

As the summit session closed, some work colleagues saw the tears in my eyes and asked if I was all right. "No," I replied, "but I believe I'm going to be." I left the summit and drove home, weeping and repenting in my car. God revived and restored a prodigal son's heart that night.

That night at the summit, God graciously and abruptly drove me to my knees, breaking my heart of stone and giving me "a heart of flesh" (Ezekiel 11:19). God could have chosen to humble me in private, but a father knows his children. Knowing exactly what would be best for me, he led me to a place of repentance in front of many of my music business colleagues—the movers and shakers of the industry.

Soon after the summit my resignation was announced. A colleague commented over lunch, "You know, you look and sound like Douglas Mann, but the words coming out of your mouth aren't his. Who *is* this person?"

I tried explaining that all I knew was that I'd heard a call to "follow me," but some of my colleagues were skeptical. "It's not like you had some Damascus Road experience, like the apostle Paul. Who do you think you are? You're not Moses leading your people to the Promised Land."

Hearing such things helped me clearly recognize I had been as guilty as they were in casting stones. How jaded we can become as Christians, to the point that when we hear stories about God calling people, we assume they must be delusional. It was painful to experience, but God gave me a depth of understanding and love for my detractors I couldn't conjure in my own strength.

I soon flew for a two-week short-term mission trip to Ireland to see the work happening there in a fledgling evangelical church community.

I heard stories of pastors' and volunteers' struggles in a country considered Christian, statistically speaking. They lamented the circumstances, yet each exuded such a sense of joy, accepting the fight and knowing God had placed them there. There was a confidence from these men and women, a sort of edgy anticipation, adrenaline combined with incredibly long-suffering faith. I wondered if maybe it was like what David had felt, slingshot in hand, beads of sweat rolling down his brow before he went out to meet ferocity in Philistine flesh.

All of this gripped my heart to where I could no longer sleep nights, sometimes waking while hearing voices, seeing faces of people calling me to come back to Ireland. I remember clearly waking with tears streaming down my face and saying aloud, "How can I not go?"

I was having a Damascus Road experience.

In light of eternity, whatever skepticism I felt seemed minor; meanwhile, this call from God was life changing, so much so that I joyfully abandoned my profitable and productive music business career, giving away my personal belongings to those in need along the way. I'd finally found the something worth losing everything for, something that ran contrary to the American dream and far closer to the gospel.

ACQUIRING A NEW APPETITE

This *something* also ran contrary to what I'd found in American churches, the "blessings" alluded to and even promised. What I experienced was how fishermen like Peter, Andrew, James and John, and a tax collector named Levi, could simply walk away from their vocations, having been prepared in their hearts and minds to respond to Jesus' words "Follow me." Like them, I felt I finally understood my life really wasn't my own to live as I pleased. And while that didn't make it easier to follow Jesus, it made it far more understandable.

Experiencing the *something* closer to the gospel meant it really isn't about me, and that this world is temporary and this life is fleeting, as every moment is. It was like my rusted iron shackles were cut and I was set free to discover freedom. When I'm asked what giving away my belongings to the poor, my sports car to charity, selling my house and walking away from a cultural Christian lifestyle felt like, I say it felt like being released from a twisted sense of duty or obligation, like giving up forever the idea of doing what good Christians do, and walking away to live out the freefall of faith. It was exhilarating because I knew modeling it before a watching world would mean I'd have to claim this new *something* over my false sense of security, showing my warts and all.

And by *exhilarating*, I mean terrifying.

Let me say I am all for working hard. I believe in accomplishing much and seeing the results from unwavering sweat equity. I also liked the security of an executive-level job, the large house in a prestigious location, the luxury of cars and a healthy paycheck. But in time I discovered I had allowed those things to become a golden calf in my life. I had been bowing down and worshiping them in many different ways big and small. The appetite to gain more can creep up bit by bit. Before I knew it, my life revolved around that appetite. Insatiable desire leads to ruin and destruction; that's exactly what Paul forewarned: "Some people, eager for money, have wandered from the faith and pierced themselves with many griefs" (1 Timothy 6:10). I had to unlearn feeding this appetite and relearn being content with what God provided for me.

Fast forward to my one-room studio apartment with its leaking roof and drafty walls, with just enough food and clothing to survive day to day. While it was a welcome respite from living in my Jeep, unlearning my old appetite was a kind of death. And relearning the promise of God's provision has been a kind of rebirth.

POWER AND SUFFERING

Through the years that followed, I learned that people who embrace the power of Christ also share in his suffering. The two go hand in hand. Suffering isn't an obligation or duty of the Christian, rather it is an honor that has been granted to us. Paul tells us as much: "For it has been *granted* to you on behalf of Christ not only to believe in him, but also to *suffer* for him" (Philippians 1:29, emphasis added). This cuts deep against the very grain of our culture: sharing in suffering is never pleasant or convenient, and so we don't naturally consider allowing it into our lives. But for Christians to avoid sharing in Christ's suffering is to attempt something impossible: sharing in his suffering is not something we can choose to opt in to or out of. It is an unavoidable gift to carry throughout our lives on this earth.

Since students are not above their teacher, just like servants cannot be above their master, some semblance of Jesus' suffering awaits us. Jesus was mocked, betrayed, spit on, beaten. I believe to the extent that we attempt to inoculate ourselves against suffering, to distance ourselves from the unpleasant implications of professing faith in Jesus, we are betraying Christ. As Jesus stood before the Sanhedrin, Peter sat in the courtyard denying with an oath, "I don't know what you're talking about. . . . I don't know the man!" (see Matthew 26:69-75). As his accusers pressed him, Peter called down curses on himself, vehemently denying and abandoning Jesus.

We do this. I do this—and there seems to be more than a little bit of Peter in all of us. If we really are Jesus' students, his servants, his followers, then a death awaits us. We must die to ourselves to move closer to what Jesus modeled in Scripture; if we are to be restored, to recover from our spiritual bankruptcy, we need to not care two straws about our earthly reputations. We need to die to ourselves.

Make no mistake: if we would follow, some sort of suffering awaits.

PRIDE, THE POWERLESS PRETENDER

War, corruption, worldwide protests, global recession, devalued currencies, unemployment, economic and individual depression, home and business foreclosures, defaulted mortgages, overdrawn bank accounts, bankruptcies and bailouts. One would think that the times we live in and the centrifugal push we experience from what feels like our world spinning off its axis create one of the greatest hurdles to living the Christian life. But that simply is not so. While there are dire and tragic circumstances in the world, the greatest obstacle to living the Christian life is actually *us*.

Our natural inclination is to avoid dealing with our sin as much as possible. Our emotional overdrafts point to our spiritual bankruptcy, and we ignore our self-righteousness, legalism, incompetence and rampant inconsistency. We refuse to acknowledge the critical spirit that ravages our hearts and lives, the presumption of our own importance, the envy, lust, fear and anxieties leaking out of our hearts.

Artists' sensitive discernment can be their downfall if they allow their pride to go unchecked.

As artists of faith, this pride inevitably causes us to undermine our work. Shame and insecurity about our art, recognizing it's not sufficiently "Christian" to ourselves or the church, and falling short of society's high standards for professional work can cause us to try to work harder in our own strength for respect and prestige. Yet from a sacred place of weakness and suffering, there is a *true* power that emerges in which we can produce works inspired by the Holy Spirit.

Ironically, we may find it easiest to ignore these obstacles to our discipleship in a confined church community. Many carefully constructed subcultures of Christendom are one-way streets; they provide a cloister where we can be safe from uncomfortable reality. The trouble is, we don't stay there. Outside their walls, we scurry to find worth in our possessions, job titles and comfortable areas of life.

Thankfully, while God is not satisfied with the lives we construct for ourselves, he continues to love us indiscriminately, understanding our humanity. He actually wants to encounter us, to call us into the life that lies on the other side of our dying to ourselves, to shower us with his indiscriminate love.

From my rooftop window in Mobile, coffee in hand, I peered over the imperfect panoramic inner-city view. Clothes hung to dry on laundry lines, strung from balcony to balcony, running from building to building. I remembered that God does not leave us when we mess up and add to our dirty laundry list. Instead, he comes to us and frees us from it.

Spiritual growth occurs not when everything is right in our world but when we are in the midst of trouble. When we don't see a way out of the tumultuous difficulty of circumstances and hope is wavering, it is the arduousness of those circumstances that shape and sharpen us like iron on iron. And here we find God comes to us, reminding us to rest in the truths of the gospel and to exercise his precepts and practice them to be transformed by their power.

FOR REFLECTION AND DISCUSSION

1. How do you define success in your life?

2. How have you experienced spiritual bankruptcy in your life?

3. Do you agree with the challenge that to freely follow Jesus, we "won't care two straws about our earthly reputation"? How has that played out in your life?

2

CALLING ALL
CREATIVE INCITERS

To avoid criticism say nothing,
do nothing, be nothing.

ELBERT HUBBARD,
In Memoriam

Finally, the big day had arrived. I had planned it all out so carefully over a short period of time. Quietly tiptoeing across creaky wooden floors in the early morning hours, I grabbed my prepacked rucksack and crept down the hallway, out the back toward the small concrete patio, careful to avoid the squeaky screen door. With beads of sweat on my brow, I slowly closed the door behind me, set off down the street and exhaled a dizzying sense of relief.

My father, mother and brothers were sound asleep. It would yet be a long time before my classmates would gather at the public bus stop to be shuttled off to school. With an extraordi-

Cold War

Cold War is highly textured, deep layers of acrylic on canvas, and a piece of art not without controversy. Some people perceive it as a political statement, but it was actually an emotive expression of my inner struggle after returning home from years of overseas ministry.

The upside-down flag is a signal of distress and represents the cultural battle played out in my heart and soul. The flag's battle-scarred, worn parts indicate the stress and weariness that come with reverse culture shock. (Courtesy of DankoArtStudio.com)

---

narily naive sense of adventure I drifted deeper into the foggy humidity of the dew-dripped dawn. I had taken to heart the words of Henry David Thoreau:

> Nay, be a Columbus to whole new continents and worlds within you, opening new channels, not of trade, but of

thought. Every man is the lord of a realm beside which the earthly empire of the Czar is but a petty state, a hummock left by the ice.[1]

Like the great Santa Maria sailing from port into uncharted waters, I was off to discover what I thought would be a remarkable and influential new world. My heart practically pounded from my chest as our less-than-middle-class home faded in the distance.

Of course, I hadn't counted on our neighbor Mrs. Elrod being out retrieving her morning paper, the *Leaf Chronicle*—really, who is up *that* early checking the mailbox? Who likewise can conclude in no time at all what a young boy is up to, lecture him in the most polite Southern way, and then encourage and convince him to march straight back home? I'm not sure if I was stunned more by her impromptu discourse or the sight of those rolled curlers in her hair and the menthol-filtered Salem cigarette loosely dangling from her lips, bouncing like a frenzied magnetic compass as she talked almost ceaselessly. Needless to say, my attempts to leave home at a very early age were in one way or another always thwarted. Looking back, I should have thanked Mrs. Elrod.

I've often wondered at this seeming insatiable impulse to *escape*. A child of the 1960s and a teen of the 1970s, I grew up in an era packed with excess and ostentatious lifestyles, which left their marks on an impressionable child like me with their radical ideas and relaxed social taboos. The phenomenon of the 1960s permeated our everyday lives, even though in my household we were largely on its outskirts.

The 1969 Woodstock Music and Arts Fair became emblematic

of the time of increased political, social and economic awareness, student movements for world peace, growing advocacy of women's rights, and a heightened sense of distrust of authority. Through civil rights demonstrations, antipoverty programs and social revolution, high idealism and widespread antagonism gestated a fractured individualism and gave birth to a self-interested counterculture. In time, it ultimately overpromised and underdelivered on the "discovery of the real self" that many icons of the time advocated.

Yet awash in this mix, I was quickly becoming the quintessential angry young man.

THE PULL OF INJUSTICE

Needless to say, a deep sense of injustice was instilled in me early in life. It continues to pull like an undertow just below the surface.

Perhaps from my experience of random physical and emotional abuse as a young boy or remembering the men in white robes and hoods blocking our station wagon, checking inside and questioning my parents, my older brother and I learned to hide early on. We laid down in the backseat, and as we were eventually waved through, I peeked back to see flames licking up a burning cross in the darkness. My eyes widened as I saw what seemed like white ghosts fading in the distance.

I recall one instance as a young teenager: our pastor, his wife and oldest son were visiting our home one Sunday afternoon. The adults chatted over coffee on the outdoor patio, enjoying a calm, beautiful spring day, the weeping willow trees gently waving in the breeze. My younger brother and I played with the pastor's son in the room we shared. Soon, the boy began to pick on my six-year-old brother, pushing and shoving him. I told him to stop, but the shoving only intensified. When my little brother lost his balance and fell, cutting his head on the bed's sharp corner, the anger inside me erupted. Grabbing the boy's collar in one hand, the back of his trousers in another, I drove him out of the house through the patio screen door, disturbing the calm setting of our parents, replacing it with the clatter of coffee cups and saucers landing on the tabletop, and me—screaming that if he ever hurt my brother again, I'd "beat your a** without mercy."

Strangely, the pastor's son didn't accompany them on future visits.

This same fire burns in my belly when I witness the rampant injustice of our world. There's no escaping them; such "bullies" torment us at every turn. And yet, as an artist, it so often seems there's nothing at all I can do about that.

DEFINING CREATIVE INCITEMENT

I was in the Republic of Ireland when that fire, what I now recognize as the drum of the "creative inciter," first began to overwhelm my heart. As an Irish citizen (my mother was Irish, and I have dual Irish and U.S. citizenship), I've learned G. K. Chesterton was right when he said of the Irish, "All their wars are merry and all their songs are sad."[2]

Where I lived in Dublin—technically, Tallaght, a suburb I once swore I'd never live in—I often got around by bus, regularly wondering whether the bus schedule was outdated or the bus itself had gone missing (which did happen now and again). One day, on what is called a "soft day" (with floating mist that never quite becomes rain but nevertheless leaves you soaked), I was waiting, with a degree of impatience, for the 49 Bus to the city center to meet friends for the "literary crawl," a walk from pub to pub formerly frequented by Irish writers. It was thoroughly enjoyable to relive the rich past in those historic halls, watching actors recite excerpts from *Finnegan's Wake, Ulysses, Dracula* and the occasional sharp-witted epigrams of Oscar Wilde. We'd knock back pints of "the black stuff" and learn about the esteemed Republican revolutionary leader Michael Collins. We'd walk part of the way home on the damp cobblestone streets, and I'd close my eyes, breathing deep the wonder of those warrior poets whose creativity seemed to now reverberate in my heart and soul.

If this was a part of my heritage, I thought, *then maybe I too was a part of this larger work of opening people's eyes to the richness of art, music and poetic words.* It was my first thought of what I now recognize would become a deeply biblical and God-inspired call on my life.

Though in God's economy *everyone* who's reborn as his new creation is a *creative inciter*, whether man or woman, artist or farmer.

Creativity is typically described as involving the use of one's imagination. It is not exclusive to artists, writers and musicians; creativity is observable in people from all walks of life who are generally inventive and resourceful, including students, engineers, architects, professors, pastors and stay-at-home parents. Some of these people may dabble in the arts, but they primarily deal with the practical side of life, navigating problems as they present themselves, ultimately coming up with successful solutions.

Incitement, from the Latin word *incitare,* means "to awaken, to bring out of sleep." The term *inciter* conjures images and words like radicals, insurrectionists, revolutionaries and rabble-rousers. While these terms may fit God's called at particular times, *inciter* can also imply anyone who leads people to change, to improve their condition. It may be parents waking their children's minds through schooling, doctors practicing medical art to restart a heart or any teacher investing in a learner, whether disadvantaged or privileged.

Creative inciters somehow bring these two values together. A reasonable definition is "someone willing to embrace the role of *risk taker*, a person willing to be an agent of change and a driving force." A creative inciter unleashes other people's creative energy through their own; their efforts culminate in positive and productive action, not negative action from false motives. It is action from truth and is essentially revolutionary in the most positive sense of the word.

NOT *WHAT IF* BUT *WHY NOT*

Creative inciters look at the world and ask many questions. Their response to the inequities and misfortunes that surround them often leads to what-if-type questions. What if a thousand people held hands and sang outside the courthouse? What if we wrapped this bridge in yellow cellophane to protest this unfair policy?

These are not bad ideas in themselves. But I don't think what-if questions usually go far enough: I believe God's creative inciters need to ask *why not*.

What if is speculative. It is generally used when suggesting an idea. As such, it's more aggressive than *why not*, which seeks to eliminate obstacles. *What if* can just as likely be a hastily thrown lawn chair to a desperate, drowning victim; it's not necessarily a bad idea, but perhaps it's not the best. Those who ask *what if* can be like someone asking a victim to accept certain terms before pulling him or her to safety; like driving up beside someone lost in the desert and asking the person to take our car for gas and pick up a drink while there. Those who ask *what if* often come with strings, hidden traps or personal baggage.

By contrast, *why not* is sacrificial. It delivers a sense of determination and considers the situation before instigating specific action. There's something energetic about *why not* and its implicit suggestion, What are we waiting for? It's not dithering or demanding. It engages people in the pivotal moment of decision, single-minded on pursuing a course of action.

Our willingness to trade *what if* for *why not* shows how concerned we are about our reputation rather than how concerned we are with change for the better. There can be, after all, negative responses to both questions. If our responses give voice to fear of criticism, we might decide to say nothing, do nothing and ultimately forsake our calling to creative incitement.

And if we're not embracing that calling, we will not be truly becoming ourselves. As Oscar Wilde famously put it, "Be yourself. Everyone else is taken." Regardless of the medium, the canvas of the creative inciter is the human condition, in all its frailty and immense distress. American author, poet and philosopher Henry David Thoreau understood that creativity begins not with the objects of our creation but with recognizing our inherently creative selves.

> It is something to be able to paint a particular picture, or to carve a statue, and so to make a few objects beautiful; but it is far more glorious to carve and paint the very atmosphere and medium through which we look, which morally we can do. To affect the quality of the day, that is the highest of arts. Every man is tasked to make his life, even in its details, worthy of the contemplation of his most elevated and critical hour.[3]

In daring to be themselves, in daring to ask *why not*, creative inciters connect to one another like links in a chain across media and even across generations.

And this is what makes creative inciters distinctly Christian—being *in the world* but not *of* it, unimpressed with the things of ordinary life, and beholden only to God for the answer to *why not?* A creative inciter must seek to have only godly motives.

Andy Crouch adds definition to the idea of creative inciters in his book *Culture Making*:

> Like our first parents, we are to be creators and cultivators. Or to put it more poetically, we are artists and gardeners. . . .
>
> The gardener looks carefully at the landscape; the existing plants, both flowers and weeds; the way the sun falls on the land. The artist regards her subject, her canvas, her paints with care to discern what she can make with them. . . .
>
> The gardener tends what has gone before, making the most of what is beautiful and weeding out what is distracting or useless. The artist can be more daring: she starts with a blank canvas or a solid piece of stone and gradually brings something out of it that was never there before. They are acting in the image of One who spoke a world into being and stooped down to form creatures from the dust. They are creaturely creators, tending and shaping the world.[4]

A FORMIDABLE DISARRAY

The world is not clean, nice and orderly, tailor made for our own creative expression. It is in a perpetual state of formidable disarray. Yet many of us imagine it to be well and good and fit to suit. And then we wonder why life doesn't work out, why we suffer.

It takes creative people to see the world for what it is, to discern the human condition. To practice creativity is to be more keenly aware of the complexity of the world, to recognize its fragile, fractured soul. It takes creative people to awaken that awareness in others. Creativity can beget creativity.

But simply acknowledging the world as a place of disarray isn't enough. We don't want to live in a world of chaos; we want to see that world transformed into something of beauty and truth. That takes creativity as well. But even more than awareness, transformation demands incitement.

THE TRUE ARTISTRY OF THE MASTER ARTIST

As a stumbling Christian, full-time ministry worker and working visual artist, I often find the different facets of my life distressingly fractured. So it was an incredible relief when the revelation dropped into my pea brain that *Jesus was an artist.* Who knows how successful he was in carpentry (my guess is he probably could have been showing in the palace before long), but Jesus was an artist in all he practiced, particularly with words. His art for story, for linking up concepts and filling them with arresting yet simple truths was masterful. And in the ways he helped others with his art, he was modeling something extraordinary and crucial for us to follow.

Christian and *artist* seemed to me, for the longest time, to be descriptors in competition with each other. My mind went to my familiar assumptions of what constituted "Christian art"—much of which was, in all honesty, restrictive, narrow minded and genuinely shortsighted. But I've come to understand that Christianity is *itself* an art; there is artistry in being Christian, which Jesus demonstrated. He was making art by his teaching and his ministry, and he was calling his followers to a similar artistry.

I've landed on a term I like for the kind of artist Jesus was: *creative inciter.* The Scriptures provide us with numerous examples of this.

Matthew 15:21-28 tells of a Canaanite woman whose demon-possessed daughter suffered so terribly that she came and knelt before Jesus pleading, "Lord, help me!" For Jesus, it didn't matter that this woman was a pagan or social outcast; what mattered most was her great faith, which he acknowledged publicly. He was moved to absolute compassion and in turn healed the woman's daughter.

In Mark 7–8 we are told of Jesus' empathy for the great crowds that followed him. He healed the blind, the mute, the crippled and lame—all those that were laid at his feet. Jesus recognized the needs of this multitude of people and called the disciples together, expressing profound concern for the people's well-being. Then, with a few small fish and loaves of bread, he miraculously fed four thousand people in one sitting.

In John 2:1-11 it is recorded how Jesus turned six thirty-gallon stoneware pots of water into wine at a wedding celebration after all the wine had ran out. Jesus told the servants to fill the stoneware pots with water, and then had them draw some out and take it to the master of the wedding banquet. After tasting the wine, the master of the banquet called the bridegroom aside saying, "Everyone brings out the choice wine first and then the cheaper wine after the guests have had too much to drink; but you have saved the best till now" (John 2:11). This was Jesus' first miraculous sign performed revealing his glory.

Jesus not only helped others practically but spiritually, through the art of storytelling. By teaching in parables he helped followers come to understand principles like wisdom, faith, righteousness, obedience and sacrifice, as well as authentic grace, generosity and forgiveness. The parable of the talents (Matthew 25) and the parable of the ten minas (Luke 19) are unforgettable demonstrations of why we are not meant to neglect and fritter away the gifts God has given us to use, why we should actively serve and contribute to the greater good on God's behalf. Rather than hearing conceptual teaching and filing it away as "good to know," in these and other parables Jesus' followers saw what these concepts looked like in the world and were motivated to become proficient in each of them.

Jesus also used transformative creative incitement in the parable of the sower in Matthew 13. A farmer went out to sow seed, and while he was scattering it, some fell along a path, some on rocky places and some among thorns. Other seed fell onto good soil where it produced a bountiful crop, far more than what was originally sown. Jesus closed his story with a call to action, if not a benediction: "Whoever has ears, let them hear" (Matthew 13:9).

He worked to creatively reveal truth, inspiring people with wonder and engaging their minds to get them out of the way of their hearts. The farmer's seed is a metaphor for the Word of God, which is generative, but only in good soil. Jesus' story is also truthful about the hardness of some people's hearts and the idolatry of others, and incites us to prepare the soil to receive the seed.

Jesus' artistry, whether in storytelling, miracles or direct teaching, was guided by his compassion for helping people and giving them what they *really needed*. And, as we know, Jesus' creative incitement wasn't limited to teaching or storytelling; he was a creative inciter through and through, and it shaped how he saw the world and why he sought to reframe reality on multiple levels. To follow Jesus is to emulate this artistry not only in our interior lives but in how we relate to others: "We want to live well, but our foremost efforts should be to *help others live well*" (1 Corinthians 10:24 *The Message,* emphasis added).

Jesus sent out his followers not only to practice the artistry of helping others but also to be creative inciters. He could have kept his creative incitement private, satisfied with inciting individuals to lead transformed lives, sequestered and bottled up.

Matthew 9:36-37 recounts the fractured human condition. "When he saw the crowds, he had compassion on them, because they were harassed and helpless, like sheep without a shepherd. Then he said to his disciples, 'The harvest is plentiful but the workers are few.'" In recounting this scene Matthew could have ended with Jesus' poignant words, but he continued in chapter 10, telling how Jesus called his disciples to himself and then sent them out to meet the needs of people.

Jesus incited people to follow him by taking up his mission, never hiding that there would be a cost to embracing the call. There is suffering inherent in the ministry of creative incitement, and Jesus is in effect saying to his followers, "Come die with me" and see how wonderful this work can be beyond any concern for self.

He now calls all of us to go and do the same. Will we respond?

THE GORY AND THE GLORY

As a visual artist, when I paint, pigment-filled brushstrokes strike the canvas, and I sense a story being revealed that describes the stories Jesus told. In a real sense I'm helping to reveal the stories the Master told me. I communicate these parables of truth on my worn, color-stained easel, imparting implicit glimpses of the gospel through my art. I sense I am participating in a kind of creative incitement.

The rules of artistry apply: to create is to give of yourself from the uniqueness of how God has made you. It is to pour yourself out, to die a little, with the hope of life on the other side of that death. I hope and pray as I pour myself out onto every canvas that this gift God has given truly honors him, and that wherever these paintings wind up, they will impart murmurs of heaven to the ears and hearts of those who experience them. I desire that their audience will be *incited* to respond and speak what they see for the world as God intends it, and to do so according to the calling he's awakening in their lives.

There's suffering in this work, sure, and glory.

Should everyone be this kind of Christian artist? I believe regardless of how we define art, those who are redeemed will inevitably be creating and reconnecting. What should we expect but that those who are truly *remade* become *remakers*? Yet not everyone will identify as an artist. Still, each Christian act is by its very nature creative if we are helping others as God intends all his regenerated ones to do. Creative inciters' lives, then, will produce art as a natural byproduct of living as we are called to live.

The glory *is* possible: to see walls crumble, strongholds destroyed, to see lamps set on stands in the darkness, revealing what was never meant to be hidden.

The creative inciters who abandon all and act when asked to "Follow me" will one day hear the phrase, "Well done, good and faithful servant."

Come. Join the work!

FOR REFLECTION AND DISCUSSION

1. What are some ways that "Be yourself, everyone else is taken" motivates and emboldens you?

2. How will you as a creative inciter embrace the role of a driving force that unleashes creative energy that reaches a pinnacle of constructive action?

3

FISHERS OF ZEN

*Follow me, and I will make
you fishers of men.*

MATTHEW 4:19 KJV

A friend of mine in the book publishing world once told me that while books like this one are a nice thought, most Christians really don't want to take up their cross and follow Jesus. Books about sacrifice don't sell.

That comment initially deterred me from venturing any further. I was reminded of what Henry David Thoreau wrote in his journal on August 19, 1851: "How vain it is to sit down to write when you have not stood up to live." Over time, however, the tension of discontent needed for art pushed me to find that it wasn't so difficult to write about what disturbed me. The struggle within my own heart between comfort on the one hand and obedience on the other compelled me to write. Obedience seemed to me to require action, whereas I'd seen I could easily

Fishers of Zen

Inspired by Matthew 4:19, where Jesus said, "Come, follow me, and I will send you out to fish for people." Fishers of Zen (as defined in chapter 3) led me to create this painting, which I still remember showing somewhat reluctantly to Francis Chan and Nicky Gumbel while I was in the United Kingdom visiting Holy Trinity Brompton Church, Knightsbridge. Not knowing what response it would receive, I explained its muse and meaning. It must have gone well since Francis asked for a framed print of the painting.

From a distance the teal background looks to be solid, yet when the viewer approaches the art the background reveals a tic-tac-toe game being played out in the church steeple windows. The outcome between fishers of men and fishers of Zen is yet to be determined. (Courtesy of DankoArtStudio.com) use my calling to art as an excuse to disengage. Typically, when we hear words like *sacrifice*, *suffering* and *death*, we tune out. When we do that, however, we fail to hear about the life that taking up our cross opens up for us.

THE TENDENCY NOT TO FOLLOW

While I was living in the Republic of Ireland, now and again I would escape the madness of Dublin and travel to Glendalough ("Glen of the two lakes") in the heart of the Wicklow Mountains. The solitude and respite of this early medieval monastic settlement of Glendalough is a special place surrounded by lush green mountains and rock that provide much needed space and solitude to clear my head and hear my heart.

The ebb and flow of the two lakes at Glendalough reminded me of when I was a young boy sitting in a small boat in the middle of a lake with my father and brothers. My mind would bob like the cork at the end of my fishing line on the lapping water's surface, lazy and carefree. Fishing was never my forte; I only ever caught floundering fellows the size of small bait. I was a free-spirited dreamer, enjoying the warmth of the summer sun on my skin and opting to study the clouds drifting above our undulating rowboat instead of paying attention to the job of actually fishing.

I preferred to become lost in my thoughts and disengage. In truth, I preferred to be a "fisher of Zen." And I do still.

For the uninitiated, Zen is a process of introspection, of rediscovery of oneself, which is sometimes referred to as "turning the eye inward." The idea is to find a transcendent wisdom that isn't obscured by self in order that freedom from natural delusions and distortions may be realized. Two components sought in a life of Zen are good karma, which is the good consequences that result from positive actions, and nirvana, a liberated state of mind that's enlightened and awakened to a place of contentment.

Sounds nice, doesn't it? In moderation, and as guided by God, there's nothing wrong with those ideas, in theory and even in practice. But too often "fishing for Zen" can become a place of disobedience, an idol of contentment and comfort where some of us Christians prefer to reside.

Like the waters lapping on the shores of a lake, there's an ebb and flow between belief and unbelief that has led me to wonder how truly willing I am, how truly willing we all are, to enter others' lives and act as genuine agents of change in the world—engaging, influencing and embracing what Jesus and Paul modeled. Jesus came to serve, not to be served. He poured out his gifts and life to the glory of God. If Jesus is truly our Master, this is the model he left for us, whether we like it or not.

As a "fisher of Zen" my tendency is to seek out a place of comfort and contentment, an abode that provides me with a delusional sense of perfect habitation, ignoring the broken world of fragmented lives that resides just outside my door. By contrast, fishers of *men* sense the need to unlock the doors of their hearts to move into the stark reality of others' lives, knowing there will most certainly be a cost and danger in doing so.

THE COMMITMENT OF FOLLOWING JESUS

When Jesus called the first disciples, he said, "Come, follow me, and I will send you out to fish for people" (Matthew 4:19). For Christians, "follow me" could well be two of the most powerful words spoken in history. They have echoed throughout all generations and time to this very moment. These words of invitation from Jesus make our hearts race.

Jesus didn't provide the disciples with a thorough, detailed ministry plan. He simply asked them to have enough faith to follow. And they did! They pulled their boats up on shore, left everything and followed him. Do you have the boldness of faith to follow the One who waits for you to respond?

Jesus knew the risks and hardship in such an invitation. He knew something of rejection and betrayal, and he anticipated that we may well face the same. So he spoke words of encouragement as well: "Do not be afraid," he told his disciples (John 14:27). He gave us words of hope and eternal promise: "I am with you always" (Matthew 28:20). He also knew that truly following him would mean we would from time to time become weary and discouraged by circumstances we encounter on the journey. So he made yet another promise: "Come to me, all you who are weary and burdened, and I will give you rest" (Matthew 11:28).

While being an artist certainly involves times of isolation, which we'll discuss later, you can't fish for "men" when you're fishing for Zen. They are direct opposites. Sure, a state of contentment in my life is desirable; it's intoxicating enough to truly delude us into believing that contentment or "spiritual comfort" is what we're called to.

We're not called to contentment, however; we're called to take up our cross and follow Jesus, to become fishers of people for the kingdom of God. Making a decision for Christ is not a one-time thing; it is a lifetime commitment.

DISPELLING THE MYTH

If indeed we are interested in becoming "fishers of people," then one of the best places to start is with authenticity—being willing to be real and honest about who we really are. And to do that requires abandoning the "Zen" of disengaged solitary comfort and dispelling the myth that we are self-contained islands who have it all together. We do not. To flourish requires others, to find contentment by being connected in relationships. God made us this way. It isn't that we shouldn't find comfort in solitude and peaceful quiet. But too often for artists, this idea—solitude and silence—can become a primary value. And soon we are not engaged with the world around us. We aren't being real with people because we aren't often enough *with* people. Being real with people requires us to dig deep, examining our motives and answering whether we truly desire others to know us or only know *of* us.

Another pitfall of Zen fishers, I've personally found, is that we try to manage what others see of us and how we're perceived. We can easily opt for being known *of* and not known. This idea works well for marketing a brand, but it doesn't sync with living out the gospel. The gospel calls on us to be *known*—by both God and others.

Why do we do this? Simple enough. To be known is costly. We run the risk of being exposed for who we really are. *Why in the world would we ever want to be so exposed?* Left to our own desires, we probably wouldn't. Yet there is an undeniable beauty in seeing the truth of someone that makes us drop our superficial façades and inspires us to embrace our weakness. When our claims to a perfect Zen persona are relinquished, the myth of having it all together is exposed for the lie it is.

Isaiah's keen awareness of his sin and God's holiness brought him to see his own need and led him to drink deeply from the cup of brokenness, of his own powerlessness.

"Woe to me!" I cried. "I am ruined! For I am a man of unclean lips, and I live among a people of unclean lips, and my eyes have seen the King, the LORD Almighty."

Then one of the seraphs flew to me with a live coal in his hand, which he had taken with tongs from the altar. . . . "See, this has touched your lips; your guilt is taken away and your sin atoned for."

Then I heard the voice of the Lord saying, "Whom shall I send? And who will go for us?"

And I said, "Here am I. Send me!" (Isaiah 6:5-8)

What Isaiah saw was a realistic view of himself and God. Only then was Isaiah ready to be to sent out and used by God. Like Isaiah, we may choose to embrace our weakness, even minister from it, with confidence that doing so reveals God's all-surpassing, sufficient grace and power working in and through us.

The apostle Paul went so far as to boast about his weaknesses so Christ's power would rest on him (2 Corinthians 12:9). He embraced not only the power but also the shared suffering in Christ, as we see in Acts 16:20-23:

They brought them before the magistrates and said, "These men are Jews, and are throwing our city into an uproar by advocating customs unlawful for us Romans to accept or practice."

The crowd joined in the attack against Paul and Silas, and the magistrates ordered them to be stripped and beaten with rods. After they had been severely flogged, they were thrown into prison, and the jailer was commanded to guard them carefully.

Ironically, owning our brokenness and weakness brings a *deeper* power and beauty that gives hope to the hopeless and makes the gospel attractive to the world. Our claim to be fallible "men" rather than masters of Zen demonstrates the true goodness of the good news. But there's a cost: we are suddenly no longer able to hide in protection behind our reputation.

This doesn't mean we give others the authority to decide how we follow Jesus. Paul puts it bluntly, "If I were still trying to please people, I would not be a servant of Christ" (Galatians 1:10). But it does mean we no longer hold any claim to the myth of being an impressive specimen.

THIS BEAUTIFUL MESS

As a visual artist, I proactively engage with my audience at galleries, showings and art events. I was once asked to show my paintings at a private home showing in which proceeds were donated to an organization fighting human trafficking. On the guest list were many Christians but also many nonbelieving neighbors of the hosts. After the hosts' introductory comments, I mingled and made introductions to the guests.

Two women were intensely studying one of my paintings. It was obvious they were partners, a lesbian couple. Few people acknowledged their presence, and it was obvious they weren't known to the larger group. I walked across the room, introduced myself and thanked them for coming. What followed was the most engaging conversation of my evening, spanning the topics of my painting, art and much of our experiences in life. I was enthralled listening to their story, what they saw in my painting and what it meant to them, and we had a great time discussing deeper questions, not skimming the surface or avoiding it entirely.

I was reminded that this is the work we do as creative inciters, plunging deeper in and swirling the water, or turning the soil of the soul over to see what might be discovered and revealed.

And I had to wonder, was it mere coincidence that it was among the "outsiders" where I found such fertile insight and connection?

Do you practice your art in a community, or are you mostly disengaged from the culture around you? Exclusively pursuing this kind of fishing for Zen will dilute our art and leave our lives comfortably numb. People of faith must resist the bait of the American dream or wind up hooked to a church culture that looks more like an outdated theme park than the kingdom of God.

When we close our eyes to the reality of life around us, the prevalence of joy and pain, our hope for the future can become fragile. We need to be purposeful. We need to stop and ask ourselves what we're choosing to see—and choosing not to see. We must enter into the tenuousness of humanity to where we no longer idealistically safeguard ourselves from the suffering and pain outside our windows. If we refuse to hear and respond to the call to be fishers of people in our world, we may want to really consider stop bearing the name of Christ altogether. Really.

We need a jolt of old time gospel and transcendental love to transform us from fishers of Zen into "fishers of men." One possible solution to our underwhelming spiritual slumber might be to lock ourselves out of church. Not permanently; maybe every other week or so for a time. It's not as though people would be kept from hearing the gospel; frankly, we've already found plenty of ways to keep ourselves from facing that. I simply reason that if we spent our "spiritual time" on people who are actually looking for something more than Zen, others would not only hear the gospel more often but more importantly they'd see it lived out. It's not wrong to "test the temperature of the water" (i.e., hot, cold or lukewarm) and lock ourselves out of the church for a time so we can find true security beyond our industrial-strength padlocks. Why not force ourselves onto the streets of our communities and into people's lives? If we chose to do this, I wonder how many of us would quietly slip around the corner when no one was looking and go back to our comforts.

STILL LIFE IN MOTION

I like to visit art galleries and museums whenever I can. I move through them at a leisurely pace, taking in all of the art possible, giving thought not only to the work itself but also to the lives behind each piece. I often wonder what the artist wants to say to me—what he or she was feeling or walking through in his or her life when creating the work.

One time at the Louvre Museum in Paris as I was sitting across the room from a still life (one of those paintings of fruit in a bowl or books on a table), I found myself marveling that, like an image in still life, I'm a piece of living history, a classic ornament suspended on a museum wall watching onlookers and time itself pass slowly by.

Suddenly, like the revelatory carpe diem scene in the movie *Dead Poets Society*, I realized that *in reality* I was nothing more than a piece of living history. And just like that painting, *I* was living a "still life." This realization grew and grew until it seemed it would swallow me whole, and left me with a kind of transcendental whiplash (thankfully it didn't leave visible marks). I lurched to the museum exit and spilled out onto the Parisian streets, making my way to the river Seine. Looking out over the river and on the beauty of Paris, an inkling of a distant desire was ignited for me to determine to lead a still life that was nevertheless somehow in motion.

We're tempted to live like we're in a still life because it's safe; nothing can upend us or disturb us. But we're not in a still life; we're living history, a story currently being written. And stories have drama and risk, plot twists and tragic turns. They also have a beginning, a middle and an end—something that is unattractive to fishers of Zen but is promised us in the Bible: there was a beginning, there will be an end, and in the meantime we are invited to live in the middle.

TRAGIC TURNS AND NARRATIVE TWISTS

I have seen and personally experienced how the twisting narrative of life can grow complicated, sometimes unmanageable. But we must learn to accept that we'll fall down at times, and we'll have to gather our wits and muster the will to rise, wipe the grime from our face and walk forward on feet of clay to move into genuine faith and hope.

Oscar Wilde said, "We are all in the gutter, but some of us are looking at the stars."[1] If I've learned anything trying to follow Jesus for more than twenty-plus years, it's that I am a fallible and broken person, fluctuating between highs and lows in a troubled and fragmented world. I have privately suffered from posttraumatic stress disorder and roamed like a vagrant through valleys of depression feeling as if I could have spiraled out of control in isolation; all while wearing an artificial veneer to mask my struggle and my real self to others. I enabled loved ones to practically drown me in their own victimization, which in time left a heart-sickening, devastating trail of tears and emotional carnage in my life and, sadly, in others' lives. I own my story of brokenness like a set of shattered plates; shards of earthenware imperfectly glued into a confusing mosaic.

Singer-songwriter Brandi Carlile sings,

> All of these lines across my face
> Tell you the story of who I am.[2]

We are what our stories have made us, which can be a devastating fact until we remember that God's story includes a happy ending that features starving beggars who find themselves on their way to a banquet with an invitation that reads, "Come just as you are."

Coming just as we are means bringing our whole past with us, and all that our past has wrought in us. It also, however, means moving toward the future promised to us by the host of the banquet, the One who went out of his way to fish for us, to catch us, to reel us out of our still life and into his better story.

> Just as I am, though tossed about
> With many a conflict, many a doubt,
> Fightings and fears within, without,
> O Lamb of God, I come, I come. . . .
>
> Just as I am, thou wilt receive,
> Wilt welcome, pardon, cleanse, relieve;
> Because thy promise I believe,
> O Lamb of God, I come, I come.[3]

Maybe these words resonate with your heart and soul, your deepest inner longings. It is that assurance that makes me strongly believe that if we actually are truthful enough with ourselves to come as we are, to go where God sends us as we are, others will be drawn to join us in the eternal celebration to come to God's banquet table.

FOR REFLECTION AND DISCUSSION

1. How does "being known of" differ from "being known"?

2. What does it mean to drink of and then minister from the cup of our own brokenness?

3. What are some of the ways you can relate to the image of an impoverished, starving beggar who happens to be on his way to the banquet table where the invitation thankfully reads, "Come as you are"?

Part Two

ART

It is not what a man does that determines whether his work is sacred or secular, it is why he does it. The motive is everything.

A. W. Tozer, *The Pursuit of God*

4

WORSHIP AS A CREATIVE LIFESTYLE

I'll bring you more than a song,
For a song in itself
Is not what You have required.

MATT REDMAN,
"The Heart of Worship"

Earbuds have become part of our cultural DNA; for many of us, they might as well be a permanent part of our anatomy.

Many of us go about our daily routines with buds in our ears. We wake with our earbuds; we sip our cappuccinos and lattes to them; we even share our lunches and snacks in unison with them. They travel with us on public transportation to our work; they accompany us through hours of work and meetings. They help us navigate the twists and turns of our day, and like a loyal pet they follow us home at the end of each workday. The very next morning it's like we hit repeat.

Colors of Ukraine

Painted from my many fond memories of Ukraine over the years: lasting friendships, *kvass*, the most incredible *borscht*, *varenyky*, cafes, working with believing and nonbelieving creatives in the arts communities. And, of course, the inspiration of the golden domes of St. Michael's Eastern Orthodox Church on the right bank of the Dnieper River, which overlooks Kiev's historical district of Podil, a part of the capital city where I often stay. (Courtesy of DankoArtStudio.com)

We imagine our earbuds surrounding us with the soundtrack of our lives. Many of us sanctify our soundtracks by pumping Christian music through our earbuds and constantly feed off worship. Worship, of course, is far more than a song; it is an intentional lifestyle.

Romans 12:1 tells us, "I urge you, brothers and sisters, in view of God's mercy, to offer your bodies as a living sacrifice, holy and pleasing to God—this is your true and proper worship." Living as sacrifices is our spiritual act of worship. We please God not when we listen to worship music but when we worship through active obedience and sacrifice. When we give of our time and our resources, when we care for the neighbor next door, the widow and orphan, the poorest of the poor—all with a vision and great hope to see cycles of physical and spiritual poverty broken and good news breaking into people's lives—then we are worshiping.

Christians seem to be highly adept at talking about this kind of worship, but finding the place of sacrifice and then dwelling in it is something we often manage to avoid. Can it be said of us what Paul said of the Corinthians: "There's no end to what has happened in you—it's beyond speech, beyond knowledge. The evidence of Christ has been clearly verified in your lives" (1 Corinthians 1:5-6 *The Message*)? Or what about the Romans: "People everywhere keep telling me about your lives of faith" (Romans 1:8 *The Message*)? As ambassadors of Christ to this world, we can't simply live off of what God has done in our lives; we are meant to invest in those around us.

CHURCH OF THE LIVING EARBUDS

We too easily find ourselves in the Church of the Living

Earbuds. But God is calling us to be the Church of the En-kindled Countenance.

The Church of the Living Earbuds is a mobile collective of sole proprietorships. Each is part of an individualized insti-tution that insulates like a Teflon coating, helping the faithful tolerate what life throws its way, and altering moods like a phar-maceutical store through apps, music, books, podcasts, games and more.

The Church of the Enkindled Countenance is not recognized by songs about love, clever slogans, symbols, tag lines, acces-sories or devices. Onlookers recognize the Church of the En-kindled Countenance by how its members love one another—and also how they love others, even the unlovable, against the canvas of a loveless and impassive culture. It's not so much what they say as it is what they do and how they do it. This is an inspired ecclesial community, one whose profile ignites flames that are encouraged, awakened, instigated and spurred into forward motion. It is a church acutely tuned to the suf-fering of the world and those around us, so much so that it is impossible to flash pearly white smiles, groomed and coiffed hairdos, and drink Evian water. Instead, this church is willing to suffer as our Savior did.

Active participants in the Church of the Enkindled Counte-nance are intensely interested in being genuine agents of in-fluence, in effecting change in their local communities and the world, in being creative inciters where they live purposely, if not passionately, in pursuit of a life that models sacrifice.

MORE THAN A SONG

Singing songs to a loving God is appropriate. Don't get me wrong.

But it's far too easy to reduce our understanding of worship to singing, or getting together to sing, once or twice a week, perhaps even only at Christmas and Easter. Worship is in reality more primal than that: it's a constant response to the overwhelming love, mercy and grace poured out on us from our heavenly Father. That we have a mediator in Christ who provides us with an eternal inheritance is more than enough to ignite some form of worship in our hearts that then seeps out from the very pores of our lives for all to see. As worship music artist Ben Cantelon once said, "Worship reminds us that God is far bigger than any of us, far brighter than any of our gloom and far more real than any of our denial."[1]

The Beatitudes, now that is worship. In the Beatitudes we are invited to embrace the characteristics of Christ.

> You're blessed when you're at the end of your rope. With less of you there is more of God and his rule.

> You're blessed when you feel you've lost what is most dear to you. Only then can you be embraced by the One most dear to you.

> You're blessed when you're content with just who you are—no more, no less. That's the moment you find yourselves proud owners of everything that can't be bought. . . .

> You're blessed when you care. At the moment of being "care-full," you find yourselves cared for.

> You're blessed when you get your inside world—your mind and heart—put right. Then you can see God in the outside world. . . .

You're blessed when your commitment to God provokes persecution. The persecution drives you even deeper into God's kingdom.

Not only that—count yourselves blessed every time people put you down or throw you out or speak lies about you to discredit me. What it means is that the truth is too close for comfort and they are uncomfortable. You can be glad when that happens—give a cheer, even!—for though they don't like it, *I* do! And all heaven applauds. And know that you are in good company. My prophets and witnesses have always gotten into this kind of trouble. (Matthew 5:3-5, 7-8, 10-12 *The Message*)

Embracing the Beatitudes, we come to understand that this life and world are not really all about us. We truly begin to live life as it was meant to be lived—which is the heart of worship.

Imagine if our lives sang back to God what he is saying to us. People would marvel at such a dialogue. When the immeasurable width and depth of Christ's love is encountered and the Spirit works in and through us, then, over time, those around us will recognize the true definition of worship.

SQUARE PEGS IN ROUND HOLES

Christians anticipate the unveiling of a heavenly city whose architect and builder is God (Hebrews 11:10). In the eyes of the world, this makes us appear odd, like square pegs in a world of round holes.

That's part of the plan, I think. Being odd, being shaped for a different setting, is one of God's acts of creative incitement: like the burning bush that roused Moses' curiosity and caused

him to come up close, Christians are meant to be artistic odd-
ities that draw others to God. Maintaining that oddness, and
keeping our oddness artistic and not just odd, is one of the
challenges of faith.

When we were children, our imaginations soared; we knew
virtually no boundaries to where our imaginations might take
us. Boundless imagination, however, is threatening to the order
of things, and so we are actively encouraged to grow out of it.
Without active resistance, over time we conform to the shape of
the boxes we are encouraged to fit into. We begin to accept the
status quo and abandon who God intended us to be.

But I don't think we ever lose a love of the freedom to be who
God made us to be. Some part of us longs to be that square peg
once again, to see our edges refined and sharpened. Our inner
oddness wants to rise up and break free from the boxes we've
been placed in. We are meant to cut against the grain, to cultivate a dynamic, positive tension around us that points people
to the good news that Christ offers.

From a Birmingham jail cell Martin Luther King Jr. captured
this positive tension when he wrote,

> I must confess that I am not afraid of the word "tension." I
> have earnestly opposed violent tension, but there is a type
> of constructive, nonviolent tension, which is necessary for
> growth. Just as Socrates felt that it was necessary to create
> a tension in the mind so that individuals could rise from
> the bondage of myths and half truths to the unfettered
> realm of creative analysis and objective appraisal, so must
> we see the need for nonviolent gadflies to create the kind
> of tension in society that will help men rise from the dark

depths of prejudice and racism to the majestic heights of understanding and brotherhood.[2]

Our fellow artists, musicians, writers and other creative inciters of faith can be models for us in this, breaking free from those conventional boxes and carving a new pattern in the fabric of the church. Unsatisfied to merely appreciate or consume, they hurl themselves into their craft with all its unpredictable discoveries, producing art that stirs and awes hearts and imaginations, and over time incites others to a similar creative engagement. And by doing so, this creative engagement and the incitement it generates spills over to others in the church and perhaps into others' lives. What a wonderful yet disturbingly diverse and unique mosaic this could look like in the body of Christ; one that is led by the Holy Spirit and orchestrated by the very hands of God.

REDEFINING WORSHIP

The heart of worship and the Christian life itself is about our focus on God; our daily encounters with him and our interactions with other people create the context of our worship. Worship should never exist to serve the Christian subculture; it should not be allowed to pay homage to a personality on a pedestal or behind a pulpit. Worship should inspire, strengthen and build the church, and lead to the transformation of individual lives, local communities and ultimately the world.

Perhaps, then, we don't need to see worship itself redefined as much as we need to change how we approach it.

In the Church of the Living Earbuds, well-intentioned, truly gifted human beings, through no fault of their own, can become venerated images, idols that *unintentionally* distract us from the one true God. It's extremely sad to see talented men and women of faith come to expect a kind of preferential treatment because a precedent had been set in motion early on with many of their predecessors. Some worship leaders approach their craft with a sense of entitlement, rather than seeing it as a ministry of creative incitement, a precursor to the church's sacrificial obedience. If we want to be the Church of the Enkindled Countenance—that square peg that oddly appeals to a world of round holes—we need to render to the worship superstars of this world what is theirs and render to God what is God's.

I have worked with a well-known Christian music artist or two in my time who would demand more money, first-class flights, even transportation in tinted-windowed Cadillac Escalades to and from performance venues. When one particular artist didn't get his way, he would actually hang up on me, an infantile act of defiance. I would listen to that tedious dial tone and wonder, *What have we become?* I have seen my fair share of self-absorption and questionable behavior in the book publishing industry as well—not to mention in mission agencies and local churches.

Juxtaposed against such disordered ministry is the life and legacy of Rich Mullins, a Christian music artist and songwriter well known for his devotion to his Lord and the enormous generosity of his charity to others. Shortly before his death in September 1997, Rich Mullins was quoted as saying,

> Jesus said whatever you do to the least of these my brothers you've done it to me. And this is what I've come to think. That if I want to identify fully with Jesus Christ, who I claim to be my Savior and Lord, the best way that I can do

that is to identify with the poor. This I know will go against the teaching of all the popular evangelical preachers, but they're just wrong. They're not bad, they're just wrong. Christianity is not about building an absolutely secure little niche in the world where you can live with your perfect little wife and your perfect little children in a beautiful little house where you have no gays or minority groups anywhere near you. Christianity is about learning to love like Jesus loved.[3]

Worship that does for Jesus what he doesn't need done, and, worse, absolves us from doing for Jesus what needs to be done—what Matthew 24 unambiguously singles out as the active care for the least of these—is not ultimately true worship. It's more like fishing for Zen, more like attending the Church of the Living Earbuds. True worship involves a woeful countenance because there are so many "least of these" within our reach but suffering our neglect. Worship is woeful countenance because until that day when God wipes every tear from every eye, God's church should vigilantly mourn with those who mourn and seek the good of those who suffer.

Being concerned isn't enough; to worship is to be compelled. Being aware isn't enough; to worship is to be moved to action. We're not in this world to make a living but to extend the hope that has been extended to us. If we forget that, we risk our own spiritual impoverishment, our own alienated hearts. We walk further down the road toward spiritual bankruptcy. I wonder what kind of good news we reveal to those in need and to a scrutinizing, skeptical world if we act out what the apostle James wrote in his letter to the church:

If a brother or sister is poorly clothed and lacking in daily food, and one of you says to them, "Go in peace, be warmed and filled," without giving them the things needed for the body, what good is that? So also faith by itself, if it does not have works, is dead. (James 2:15-17 ESV)

How many of us would be comfortable to have the apostle Paul walking among us today, looking here and there, poking around in places we think he shouldn't be? What a mess that inciter would make. Would he say to us what he said to the Athenians: "I see that in every way you're very religious" (Acts 17:22)? I think Paul would adamantly remind us that God doesn't live in temples built by human hands, and that we're not meant to follow the ways of this world. Why? Because God lives in us; we are his workmanship, created in Christ to do good works for God's kingdom, not for our own self-sufficient fiefdoms.

Connected Churches is a Seattle-based organization working to network and connect church leaders with artists, writers, musicians and other creative inciters, assisting them to engage in conversations that will lead to actual change, change prompting positive and productive creative action from truth and godly motives.

Wade Olinger, executive director of Connected Churches, is leading the initiation of these conversations to cultivate environments of true worship, those of authentic creative incitement. This is generating a greater sense of openness and flexibility by everyone involved where churches are collectively sharing resources instead of operating individually, and returning many to live sacrificially and adopt the call to come die with us.

LIVING WITH INTENTION

As creative inciters we may want to consider not only living with intention but also pressing forward into *intentional tension*. Intentional tension is synonymous with creative incitement. When our resolve is so acutely purposeful, pushing and pulling, it creates forces that act in opposition to each other—like a tug of war. While reactionary, violent tension is not good, the intentional creation of tension can bring about dramatic transformation, as evidenced in the civil rights movement, the Reformation, the martyr tradition and, yes, even the turning of tables by Jesus in the temple.

We know and understand that we're created in God's image, but do we *really* believe that we are? What does that look like in each of our lives, and how does that play out and move forward? Implicitly, God is a creator, not a duplicator. So as our heavenly Father's children, wonderfully made in his image, why would we not model this in our own lives by living an intentional yet creative lifestyle, which can't be judged in a short time frame but rather becomes apparent over seasons of time?

Christians everywhere can apply an intentional lifestyle of creativity throughout our week. The clerk at your local grocery that you have always wanted to say something to but haven't? A work colleague suggesting that you meet over a coffee? These are opportunities to practice the art of conversation with others and to move into their lives. Though our lifestyles look the same, how we shape the expression of the creativity that flows from our lives will look different. In doing so the church truly becomes the church, a vivid snapshot of uniqueness and diversity; a body made up of different parts, skill sets and gifts—a work of art that incites people to worship.

I lived for a while in a part of Dublin that few tourists ever see, where burning and smoldering cars are standard fare and the occasional gangland-style assassination occurs. From time to time I would walk these streets noting the historic buildings boarded up and decorated with graffiti and engaging street hustlers in conversation. When you rub shoulders with people, you may or may not be prompted to share the gospel directly. But you are a part of their lives. When I was with the Irish arts team (which later branched out into Prague and the United Kingdom), it wasn't a Christian enclave. It was imperative that we invite the community in and use our art to discuss the tensions that exist in the community and the world at large. Of course, we also addressed the complications of doubting and struggling to believe. We established the arts team on the philosophy of being in the middle of the culture.

Traversing overseas to many different cultures on ministerial expeditions in cafés, pubs, hostels and streets (with some sense of nomadic wanderings) has, in a sense, become my own sacrifice of praise, giving glory to God by inciting something where God had put me. I'm not a risk taker or adrenaline junky, but because Jesus pressed into the lives of others by keeping company with people who were undesirable or written off as sinners, extending them the cups of grace and hope—because he so consistently showed such people glimpses of the gospel— how can I not do the same?

To worship God in spirit and truth is to get our hands dirty and uncomfortable, to move into the brokenness of people's lives. Artistry is like that—a little messy most of the time and extremely messy now and again. But we're called to a gospel artistry, called to live out the gospel in practical ways, to creatively incite people toward life in Christ. Gospel artistry starts with the willingness to show up, allowing your heart—your self—to be available and vulnerable to those around you. As we do that, we become gospel artists, but more than that, we become an image of his work of art.

FOR REFLECTION AND DISCUSSION

1. How do you approach worship in your life: As an experience? As a ministry? As a lifestyle? Explain.

2. What are some ways you can intentionally introduce creativity into your worship lifestyle?

5

BEYOND PROPAGANDA
AND BOXES

*The job of the artist is always
to deepen the mystery.*

FRANCIS BACON

In the early morning hours when the light of day hasn't yet fallen on the cityscape and its concrete labyrinth, I sometimes drive to work to get an early start on the day. That requires driving past cardboard boxes that litter the downtown streets. These make-shift homes evaporate in the morning sunlight like dew on the grass; any thought of the displaced persons that fill them fades like a well-timed and welcomed amnesia.

One early spring as I was visiting Kiev, Ukraine, two of my friends made the ill-advised decision to squeeze themselves into a rusty, Soviet-era elevator with several locals from the ram-shackle apartment complex where we were staying. Moments after the elevator doors closed behind them, it shifted and ground

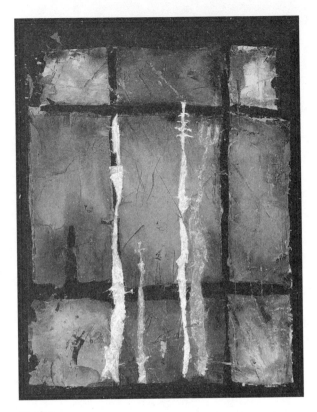

Stories

We all have more than our fair share of stories that have unfolded throughout life. This painting reflects one season in my own. Like much of my art, this piece consists of dual iconic meanings. For instance, the long knife on the left is derived from the time I was stabbed on the street as a young man, but it also symbolizes the piercing of Jesus' side while on the cross. While the cross stands for this, it also represents my faith.

The tall antenna reflects an attentiveness to see glimpses of the gospel and communicate the good news, but it also depicts those who are searching for truth. A green pitchfork on the right-hand side is a reminder that sin desires to master me and constantly poke me in my derriere. *Stories* is a very organic and earthy mixed media piece of art with heavy texture and structure combined with multiple layers, tones and colors. (Courtesy of DankoArtStudio.com) noisily to a complete halt, locking them with total strangers inside that small iron box. They were packed like a can of herring.

More than two hours later, everyone was freed, thanks to a not-so-prompt and slightly annoyed maintenance worker. From that time forward, all of us chose to skip the elevator and hike the never-ending stairwell to and from our rented flats.

Boxes are everywhere. Some are imposing and permanent, like an unreliable Soviet-era elevator. Others are temporary and tragic, like those that house human beings on the moonlit streets of Mobile, Alabama. And some boxes are receptacles for the things we don't quite know what to do with. Like God.

Like most people, I like to keep God similarly confined—there for all to see in the dim shades of gray light, but conveniently disappearing in the blistering pace of work and demands of the day.

OUTSIDE THE BOX

Why do I try to confine God to a box? I could justify excuse after excuse, but I believe it's because doing so makes God more manageable for me. A boxed in God makes convenient drive-by appearances in my life and doesn't require much of anything from me.

Ironically, when I box in God, my heart and faith are themselves boxed in—which affects my art and life, and the expression of faith that flows from it. Boxed art really leaves little to the imagination, reeks of propaganda and mediocrity, and leaves skeptics all the more skeptical.

While working in full-time ministry, I was involved in a severe auto collision, which forced me from overseas work, left me unable to play guitar and involved a grueling recovery process of physical therapy. Never would I have dreamed that this collision would be akin to a creative collision in that it helped lead me back to my art again, the visual art and creative landscape I exited from early on in college. Rediscovering painting was not only healing and therapeutic, it became my creative outlet and something I could do relatively pain free. Over time it led me to wrestle with what it meant to be a Christian producing art, and what that art should or shouldn't be, but also what it could or couldn't be. If we're being honest, we could more than likely never fully define what art that is Christian looks like or even actually is. There are those that have a strong opinion as to what they think it *should* look like (maybe you're one of those persons), but to arrive at a comprehensive definition is futile—convenient for us, maybe, but probably disappointing and even annoying to God.

As author Steve Turner writes in *Imagine: A Vision for Christians in the Arts*,

> One of the great hindrances to the development of biblically informed mainstream art has been the perception that Christians should make "Christian art" and that "Christian art" is always explicitly religious. Understood in this way, "Christian art" is not distinguished by a regenerated outlook on the whole of life but by a narrow focus on Bible stories, saints, martyrs and the individual's relationship with God.[1]

It's helpful to remember that the Bible itself is actually artful: one-third of Scripture, for example, is actually poetry. Art that limits itself to representing, even reproducing, the content of the Bible is like boxed art—derivative, burdened with propaganda, a pale reflection of the original. Truly Bible-inspired art, like a truly Bible-inspired life, will not be marked by mediocrity but will be itself creative, transforming how its audience perceives the world and even inviting the audience into its own creative act.

Given the artfulness of the Bible, we begin to see how God uses imagination to guide and teach us. The imagination we've been given is a powerful resource; the arts have served to uncover truth across cultures, becoming a kind of universal language. There's a well-known truth that says if reason gives us truth then imagination gives us meaning.[2] Imagination is what enables truth to be meaningful.

Unfortunately, some churches are languishing without access to the meaning that imagination gives us. Too many churches have pigeonholed what it means to be an artist, to be a creative inciter, by either defining what is art or what is Christian. They see art within the church as a means of evangelism—marketing.

Defining Christian art in such ways *discourages* creativity among artists. Limiting art to predetermined boundaries stifles its impact; a one-way conversation results, and we are no longer willing to enter into dialogue with one another.

Ultimately, each artist must define what makes something art. Yet at the foundation, art that's Christian will be transformative and inciting as a matter of course. Ultimately, there is no difference between making art and living artistically; both are inspired acts of response to the holy, creative Spirit within. One leads to the other, and finished works are the culmination, the bubbling over of an artist living in contact with their muse, in isolation and in community.

If we actually believe that Jesus was a creative inciter, then why would we not follow in his footsteps? Imagine what it would be like if artists of faith were invited and truly encouraged to create art as authentic, relevant expressions of faith, rather than as artifacts of propaganda. What if artists and creative inciters approached and revealed truth and beauty from indirect angles, through metaphor and mystique, understatement rather than overstatement? What if their work evoked more questions that led to truths rather than providing expeditious answers that avoided any hint of intrigue? What if they spread seeds of truth not only through their work but also their lives? In essence, they would be living out the gospel, responding to God's unremitting creative nudge.

Such an invitation sounds bold; it also sounds unusual. It's not been the lived experience of most of the creative inciters I've come to know throughout the years. They would respond in one of two ways: like children riddled by the sugar-induced effects of candy, wildly tearing away wrapping paper from gifts found beneath a festive Christmas tree, or cautiously, skeptically, suspiciously—cynical about the actual intent.

NOT SO FAST-FORWARD THINKING

I think most of us would agree that Jesus was a creative inciter. So why isn't that necessarily true of us—in our own lives or in the church? While we're often responsive to the arts, it's uncommon for us to be forward thinking enough to allow artists the freedom to be themselves—uniquely innovative, capturing imaginations once again like Michelangelo during the Italian Renaissance, or Johann Sebastian Bach engaging culture inside and outside of the church walls. Why is this so?

Innovation and forward thinking can be unpredictable, out of our control and not always safe. It's our natural inclination to want what is safe, predictable and controlled. But that inclination is not exactly biblical and actually has little to do with exercising faith. That type of white-knuckle control, in fact, throws out the whole notion of faith as being confident in what we hope for and assured about what we do not see (Hebrews 11:1).

In many major cities throughout Eastern Europe, there are miles of streets lined with towering gray apartment buildings that resemble arms stretched, reaching upward to the sky. It's as if the buildings are crying out for what they themselves prohibit—expansiveness, openheartedness, connection—corresponding to an analogy Jesus used, "If they keep quiet, the stones will cry out" (Luke 19:40). This kind of visible impression provides a vivid correlating image of how easy it is to fall into withdrawing to a secluded place within a controlled environment. If we're not creatively engaging one another, then the gospel becomes *very* small. The church settles for something far less than what it and its surrounding communities could have, and only continue to isolate and encourage artists, writers, musicians and creative inciters to work apart from them.

In the eighteenth century the Age of Enlightenment swept through western European culture, even crossing the Atlantic to the American colonies with the force of a growing tsunami that gathered strength over time. At the core of this furious storm were humanism and rational analysis, which questioned tradition, morals and customs through intellectual and scientific authority, ultimately dividing the arts, science, government and the church. We seem to have never quite recovered from the magnitude and effect of that philosophy. What a unique and powerful collaborative partnership the church, creative inciters and artists can share, however, if they choose to engage each other with respect and truly understand the common ground of the gospel that they share. If this kind of genuine recognition and relationship is facilitated, both will come to better understand one another and the truths of the gospel, and convey those truths outward into local communities and then the broader world.

THE WINDS OF CHANGE

But the winds of change gently whisper. Something is simmering just beneath the surface of society which may well signal and one day lead to historic defining moments. This could actually be a time when God ushers in a dynamic revolution through one of the more creative generations we have seen in some time; a cultural movement with a prophetic voice that pushes worship forward, ultimately leading to a spiritual movement that provokes real-life change and cultural renewal in individual lives, churches and communities around the world.

As founder, creative director and board member of International Arts Movement, internationally renown Japanese American visual artist Makoto Fujimura is a visionary creative inciter guiding a growing global community of artists and creatives to purposefully and fully integrate faith and humanity into their art. This community longs to be part of a greater story, seeing past the trivial to the transcendent. Cultivating an environment to wrestle with questions of art, faith and humanity, International Arts Movement inspires through exhibitions, workshops, screenings and performances from their New York City space.

Another visionary creative inciter is musician Daniel Bashta. Pushing the boundaries of worship and music forward is only part of who Daniel is and what he does; it's one facet of his personal expression of worship. He and his wife, Taylor, believe that worship should always be in motion, compelling us to move forward into action, and never allowing the passion and rawness of what God is orchestrating inside each of us to be diluted.

My God's not dead, He's surely alive
He's living on the inside, roaring like a lion. . . .

They started a global nonprofit mission, GoMotion Worldwide, which facilitates music, media and missions. Daniel and a growing gathering of others at RiverStone Church near Atlanta believe that since the Creator of the universe resides in our hearts, we should lead the way in culture, inspiring others to dream the dreams of the One longing to roar in and through us.

Let Heaven roar
And fire fall
Come shake the ground
With the sound of revival.[3]

There are groups of Christians in pockets of the world connecting to work together, encountering the power of God, following him, forging ahead with a vibrant vision, and reaping the empowerment of creativity not only in the arts but also in their ministries. Movements like International Arts Movement, GoMotion Worldwide, Jesus Culture, Bethel Music, Passion, Journey Church, and Charlie Peacock's Art Houses, all of which emerged from local church contexts, are leading the way in new expressions of worship. They continue to transform the landscape for artists, writers, musicians and other creative inciters. These creative worship movements foster more imagination and artistry than church leaders would have allowed in the past.

There isn't any secret formula or patented method to this, simply the recognition of what they share, the courage to close the gap and the purposeful search for ways to move forward together in faith. They understand that worship flows from all aspects of our lives, and that worship without action equals an ineffective and dead faith.

Leslie Jordan and David Leonard of All Sons & Daughters are on staff at Journey Church in Franklin, Tennessee. They are worship leaders but also part of a creative team comprising other musicians, visual artists, designers and pastors. Together, this team sketched out a creative path for their church community that encompasses all kinds of worship expressions. Over time this has included prayer, visual art, music, prose, design, writing, Scripture and even silence. The Journey Church has discovered that music is only one of the ways to express worship, and by integrating their church community into the process they now experience a greater sense of freedom in worship.

According to research from Connected Churches, many younger lead pastors recognize new approaches to worship from the younger demographic and wholeheartedly support these expressions through the use of third spaces or additional events that include meshing spoken word, visual art and music to encourage more holistic worship to organically grow.

Is this all that surprising? Whenever Christians apply their artistic talents to God's call to help others, creative incitement is always the result. For Christians have a different definition of what art is: with the Creator, as the prophets of old, calling people to join the great remaking to reconnect us through the creation of new life.

CREATIVE CONFESSION

While living and working overseas in full-time ministry, I worked with worship leaders and teams in Ireland and Ukraine. I always encouraged them to resist the "plug and play" mentality: "It came from the States or United Kingdom, so it's got to be *the way* to do it." While it's all right to be influenced by other songwriters and songs, and to truly appreciate them, I challenged them to not simply imitate gifted songwriters and worship leaders; it's equally if not more important to learn to place a distinct personal signature on it. Why? Because imitation doesn't allow for freedom of expression or anything new to emerge; keep the core of the song recognizable, but consider that worship may be meant to be an indigenous expression. Leading worship should include creating new songs to sing to God.

I like to think that the arts are confessional platforms for artistic types—some blatant, others more or less oblique, but all digging deep below the surface of life, probing beyond the ordinary and mundane, unearthing and divulging insight and meaning. In this respect, artists and creative inciters are like the conduits of creativity. They should be free to encourage one another in their creative development and spiritual journey, learning to serve and positively influence a turbulent culture of which they are a part.

Francis Bacon's insight that "the job of the artist is always to deepen the mystery" has always intrigued me, but only deepening the mystery itself and not allowing people to search for and find truth and wonder denies them an essential component in the process of discovery. In a 1992 interview singer-songwriter Suzanne Vega recognized part of this process: "All the mysteries of life come in A minor." The interviewer, Paul Zollo, goes on to say, "She had been struggling with ways to harmonically expand her music. . . . It's a struggle she's known for years, wanting to write songs that uniquely express her own soul and reveal the mysteries of life."[4]

The apostle Paul sees deepening the mystery as part of the apostolic task: "Pray for us . . . that God may open a door for our message, so that we may proclaim the mystery of Christ" (Colossians 4:3). The role of every Christian, not simply artists, is to never avert our eyes, ears or hearts from the world around us. In this respect we are all creative inciters, deepening the mystery through our art and life, communicating a revelation of truths, revealing the beauty and wonder that are an integral part of the mystery of Christ.

It could be that our own lives, like the arts, can draw people in and widen their imaginations, peeling back the layers of mystery to reveal grace, mercy and hope. Instead of allowing society to shape our thinking, we may want to take into consideration how to use the imagination and innovation God has given us to shape our circles of influence. Rather than standing *outside* the institutional church, we might see ourselves as extending the church's boundaries, working *toward* the kingdom, united in our creative work by the gospel.

A SHARED EXPERIENCE

While art created for the church is vital, creative inciters in the church need to also engage with like-minded persons who don't necessarily share their beliefs. Art can be the permeable medium between the church and world that's so desperately needed. It can move us from the safety of what has become all too familiar and help artists of faith better understand their own work and beliefs. But it can also provide nonbelieving artists the opportunity to belong to a community instead of feeling that they must first believe in order to belong. Opening our own lives to others requires vulnerability, which allows God to chip away at the cautionary walls of our hearts.

We're told in Galatians 5:6 that "the only thing that counts is faith expressing itself through love." That call to action demands a life-changing response from us. While it's natural for artists to pour everything within them into their art, they must not stop there. They could conceivably also pour themselves into others' lives too. Both ultimately are exercises in faith.

This relational outpouring is why I thoroughly enjoy attending and participating in art exhibits, music and arts festivals, and also house concerts. I like to approach groups of people viewing art at exhibits and festivals, and ask them what they see, or, after taking in a music concert, what they heard. Hearing the contrasting perceptions and views expressed is like unearthing artifacts, clues to their life stories. If I listen with my heart, not just my ears, I can often connect with them to reveal a passing presence of my faith.

WHO IS WRITING THE SCRIPT?

Whether we realize it or not, every moment of every day we're writing the script of our lives chapter by chapter, choosing what matters most to live for, influencing those around us and determining what we will be remembered for. Two important questions emerge: How do we want the chapters of our lives to read? And what are the implications of our script in light of eternity?

In 1 Corinthians 12:4-7, Paul lays out a vision for how different creative inciters will approach their roles in specific ways.

> There are different kinds of gifts, but the same Spirit distributes them. There are different kinds of service, but the same Lord. There are different kinds of working, but in all of them and in everyone it is the same God at work.

85

> Now to each one the manifestation of the Spirit is given
> for the common good.

God gives us our ministry to use within the gifting the Spirit brings. In music, in visual arts, in literature, dance and theater there is the same ministry of this single Spirit, and every day we have the opportunity to live as real examples of those who are working out our unique gifts with passion for the giver of all good things.

The church needs listeners in its body: ears that hear and mouths that speak of the wonders cultivated in private communion with God, as well as hands and feet to take these wonders produced and deliver them to the wider culture. To a deafened Christian culture, artists' works can speak of the myriad ways God engages with a fallen creation and broken world.

THE ALL-IMPORTANT QUESTION

An all-too-common default response to the first question (What script is God trying to write with my life?) is to repeat clichés or pseudospiritual answers. The better response—the response of the creative inciter—is to examine our hearts, mull over the questions, consider them in the context of our real life, and resolve to do whatever hard work comes from that process. Everyone lives by some degree of faith, wrestling with questions, doubts and inner longings. We share this in common with all kinds of people from different walks of life, ethnic, racial and religious backgrounds. When we ask these questions, we find ourselves together in a messy studio, a shared workshop of spirituality.

I was sitting in a Dublin café in the city center arts district of Temple Bar, enjoying a cappuccino, blueberry scone and sorely needed banter with a musician friend in between recording studio sessions, when he abruptly shifted the conversation to a more serious tone: "What made you leave your music business executive job and come to Ireland when most everyone here would want to leave?"

I was caught off-guard by his inquisitiveness and openness. I talked about how pivotal it was for me to take an inventory of my own life, to assess what was really important and come to terms with what I would want to be known for when I draw my last breath. "When my life is all said and done," I explained, "I want to be able to look back at my choices, and know that all that I left behind is with as little to no regret as possible. This meant if I were to be truthful with myself that I had to recognize the fact that my identity was forged and found only in my work, and outside of that, I was a hollow shell of a man."

This world is only temporary, like a single sound wave oscillating on one immense eternal reverberation. My conversation with my friend that day reminds me of Jesus' interaction on the road to Emmaus with two of his followers shortly after his resurrection. Jesus explained how the Scriptures foretold everything concerning him. It wasn't until Jesus took some bread and gave thanks, however, that their eyes were opened and they recognized him. When Jesus disappeared from their sight, they remarked to each other, "Were not our hearts burning within us while he talked with us on the road?" (Luke 24:32).

There's an implied *question* at the heart of the gospel message that's beyond words—something that unearths our deepest longings and fills that indescribable empty space within us. That's the domain of art: not so much about getting and providing solid answers as leaning in to an encounter with Jesus.

Life, like art, is a shared experience. All we can do is to expect not to have all the answers, hope to ask the right questions and move bravely into the brokenness of people's lives. As that happens, a world full of mystery, truth, beauty and wonder opens.

As Leo Tolstoy wrote, "A man who professes the teaching of Christ is like a man carrying a lantern before him on a long, or not so long, pole; the light is in front of him, always lighting up fresh ground and always encouraging him to walk further."[5] The art of faith is a developing journey that lights up fresh ground for us and those we encounter, and encourages us to walk further, alone and together, down new paths of reconciliation, redemption and restoration.

FOR REFLECTION AND DISCUSSION

1. How would you define "art that is Christian"?

2. In what ways can definitions of Christian art put God in a box?

3. While reading this chapter, what are some ways you thought of to engage more actively in creative incitement in your immediate community?

4. How are you thinking differently about the role you're to play as a Christian artist in the circles God's placed you in?

6

THE FREEDOM TO
CREATE DANGEROUSLY

*Beware of artists. They mix with all classes of
society and are therefore most dangerous.*

QUEEN VICTORIA

Several years ago, I was meeting with a friend of mine who is a pastor in Dublin. We started talking about a particular musician. "If he were ever convicted of being a musician," my friend asked, "do you think he would die an innocent man?"

There was a brief moment of silence and then we burst into laughter at his slagging of our friend.[1]

Was this a profound moment at the time? Not at all, we were just having a go at a mutual friend. Is it profound for me now? Emphatically yes, especially as it relates to allowing artists, musicians, writers and other creative inciters in the church to experience the freedom to live and create dangerously, to innovate and not vegetate in whatever walk of life they find themselves.

Not So Divine Intervention

Inspired by the French philosopher Blaise Pascal's quote, "God made man in his own image, and man returned the compliment," I painted a kite floating aimlessly in the breeze above a church steeple. Antennas atop the city buildings signify people attempting to dial in, searching through their circumstances of life for a greater sense of truth and beauty. (Courtesy of DankoArtStudio.com)

DYING INNOCENT

What if you were to ask yourself, *If I were ever convicted of being an artist, writer, musician or a creative inciter, would I die an innocent man or woman?* What would your response be?

How about the creative inciters you lead? Would they die innocent men and women? Are you, and they, living dangerously out of your freedom in Christ? Or are you, and they, trapped in a box?

To lead means to guide, to be a route or means of access that results in something. Are we leading with intention and purpose, or are we meandering, only avoiding opportunities for cultural collision?

As God's people, perhaps we have lost some of our vision, our ability to dare to dream, to shape the future without settling for someone else's definition of what that looks like. While we can have certainty about who we are in God, uncertainty is the task of creative inciters: we must push back against the status quo.

How exciting it must have been to be an artist or patron of the arts in the Victorian era of the 1800s and have Queen Victoria say, "Beware of artists." Imagine regularly rubbing shoulders with all different types of people from all classes of society and diverse beliefs and values. Personally, I would have celebrated the queen's scorn far too much with my artistic friends, and I probably would have landed in jail. Today, however, it seems that we are mostly just ignored.

Do you have some sense of affinity for this? As a creative inciter, you can have a tremendous impact on those around you, influencing hearts and lives by serving in a sacrificial, biblical way. Paul said that "Christ has set us free to live a free life. So take your stand! Never again let anyone put a harness of slavery on you" (Galatians 5:1 *The Message*). This implies that God trusts his people in the freedom he has given them. Freedom is not just a nice, warm and fuzzy concept, but an actual biblical principle.

My first winter in Ireland I learned that Irish homes are heated in only one room. Other rooms were so cold that I could see my breath. We were never warm enough. The Victorian-era windows would frost over from the inside; with my finger I would etch reversed letters and doodled drawings to be seen from the street. Too many of us are like those Irish homes; we've allowed ourselves to grow cold and become frost-covered. We etch messages in frosty windows with the vain hope that someone will notice. We forget that we are free.

Fear of freedom can rob us of ambition and dreams; it can make us backpedal and drive us back to what we perceive to be safety. God is calling us to explore, to fail, to learn, grow and flourish from each experience, knowing that he is our refuge and strength, and that he comes to be with us and help us.

JESUS ALONE

Art, to *be* art, must deal with real life; it must be made in contact with the real world. When creative inciters make art, it will be in the *isolation* of the one relationship above all—that of creator to Creator. That isolation is where every meaningful artist is filled in order to overflow from the heart to others. And any Christian artist who has ever created recognizes that he or she does so in this very particular isolation—whether holed away for months in a cabin in the woods or merely "alone" in the mind—sojourning to a "quiet place" to explore the unexplored and find what's unshared to reveal healing and help.

There must also be time for engagement with the outside

world. But every artist's creative process must cultivate an essential isolation from outside influences—even spiritually insightful and meaningful ones—or the result will be diminished, corrupted and less meaningful. No one can hear the muse on the battlefield but in the silence afterward, and this was modeled for us by our Savior who constantly went off to be alone with God.

In Mark 1:12-13 Jesus went into the desert to spend forty days alone with God to pray. And in verse 35: "Very early in the morning, while it was still dark, Jesus got up, left the house and went off to a solitary place, where he prayed."

In Luke 6:12, before calling his disciples, "Jesus went out to a mountainside to pray, and spent the night praying to God." After feeding the five thousand, he withdrew to be alone with God. When he hears his cousin John the Baptist has been killed, he goes to be alone. Jesus brought friends to the Garden of Gethsemane, but withdrew to be alone with God. What did he model? In Mark 6:31, during a very busy time, Jesus said, "Come with me by yourselves to a quiet place and get some rest."[2]

ISOLATION AND THE SPRIT

Therefore, there is no condemnation when creating out of a sincere response to the Creator, whether within a studio, a bar, an asylum or a slum in Ecuador. The indwelling Spirit overrules all law, binding those bound in love and faith to the original Inciter of all life. All artists, musicians, painters, sculptors, writers, weavers, chefs, architects, game designers, systems specialists, surveyors require solitude, some of them intense isolation for inspiration. To lean in and listen more closely, almost like eavesdropping on a conversation, they must cultivate that undistracted observation and then create.

Christian art is not primarily a matter of subject or form (e.g., biblical imagery and worship music), but a posture toward the world that bridges the divide between Creator and creation, flowing out of God's mission for us. This is the art produced, and this is the correct starting place for any Christian artist. Of course, while Christian art is not merely a "posture," it is where we begin, and this originating point for all Christians rejects the assumption that all Christians must be directly active in a particular type of "missions work." The permission granted all Christians, whether intentionally creative and artistic or not, is the new law of grace in Christ. Let no person presume the place of the guiding of God's Spirit.

In our current Christian subculture such freedom is rare. Christian creators are desperate for support of their personal and intensely isolating practice of restricting themselves and being removed from the larger culture. However, listening and acting on the Holy Spirit's leading must be the core for creative incitement, whether in active sharing or receptive listening. There is a time for creating in the atelier, and there's a time for sharing one's art, whether through missions work, gallery shows or collaborative worship sets. And the Holy Spirit's guidance is the crucial factor for creative inciters, determining when it's time for active engagement and when sustained receptive listening is required.

SHAPING THE FUTURE WITH A HAMMER

How refreshing it would be to see artists of faith considered dangerous to the powers that be because they're actively involved, engaging and influencing the society around them. Bertolt Brecht said, "Art is not a mirror held up to reality, but a hammer with which to shape it."[3] There is value, of course, in holding a mirror up to everyday life; by doing so we can reveal the frailty and starkness of the human condition. But the more dangerous art of faith involves picking up a hammer.

Each creative inciter's hammer is part of the great mystery, but it is to a great degree the life you lead, the words you write from the depths of your heart that inspire others: the lyric and melody of a song longing to be heard, your paintbrush wielded with emotion and faith across a canvas, a moment in time captured through your camera lens that needs no words yet leaves us in awe, the dance you dance first and think about later. It is every creative nail driven by your hammer that fastens rivets of truth into the alloy of life. It's this incredible sense of spontaneity in the creative process that is both immensely passionate and powerful.

Once our hammer is known to us, we must bring it to bear and employ it passionately. Use it differently than ever before. Disregard what others expect or think. We are not part of an exclusive club; we're part of something much bigger than that. And as a creative inciter, you have a unique calling and crucial role in helping others to discover this.

DISENGAGED INFLUENCE

Damon of Athens, one of Plato's contemporaries, said, "Let me write the songs of a nation and I care not who writes its laws." That's the voice of a person who understood the power and magnitude of the arts to nudge, influence and ultimately shape culture.

The apostle Paul also understood the importance of engaging and influencing from the center of culture, living a life that intentionally works outward toward the edge of it. In Acts 17, Paul keenly observed and came to understand Athenian culture to such a degree that he effectively engaged the most influential philosophers and thinkers of their day in the council meeting of the Areopagus, a place where the latest ideas were debated in Athens. Paul also engaged the Jews in the synagogue and people in the marketplace, and although some dismissed his message of good news, we're told that some believed and became followers. And his ministry to the Thessalonians reflected not just giving the gospel to a culture but, more importantly, living it out among them: "Because we loved you so much, we were delighted to share with you not only the gospel of God but also our lives as well" (1 Thessalonians 2:8).

For far too long Christian artists have taken the opposite approach, dabbling on the periphery of culture, engaging from the outward edge, pedaling as fast and furiously as we can toward the center. While we may have seen a significant influence of the gospel across the breadth of American culture, I wonder if we would find any lasting substantive depth below its surface.

The parables of Jesus are a striking contrast to contemporary Christian art. Devised and crafted from the center of culture (rather than from the sacred space of the temple), Jesus' parables invited people into the power of story, of song, of art, creating space for conversation, vulnerability, intimacy and relationship. Jesus' art was the first word in his sharing of the gospel; contemporary Christian art too often feels obligated to offer the last word, and it suffers as both art and gospel as a result.

Fear of asking questions is, at the end of the day, a lack of faith. Martin Luther King Jr. recognized the attributes of fear and resistance to change:

> [Jesus] knew that his disciples would face a difficult and
> hostile world, where they would confront the recalcitrance of

political officials and the intransigence of the protectors of the old order. He knew that they would meet cold and arrogant men whose hearts had been hardened by the long winter of traditionalism. . . . He gave them a formula for action, "Behold, I send you forth as sheep in the midst of wolves." . . . "Be ye therefore wise as serpents, and harmless as doves." . . . We must combine the toughness of the serpent with the softness of the dove, a tough mind and a tender heart.[4]

To blatantly spell out a simplistic message of the gospel and the mystery behind our lives is like digging holes to the reach the sky. It denies people the all-important process of discovery and the opportunity for us to walk alongside them in this as they discover the glorious gift that Paul speaks of: "Where the Spirit of the Lord is, there is freedom" (2 Corinthians 3:17). Through imagination and creativity, we *can* point others to this great mystery of freedom—to Christ.

Revolution NYC, a unique ministry founded by Jay Bakker, offers an open and inclusive forum for the process of discovery. Featuring art exhibits, DJs, bands and guest speakers tailored to the interests of the surrounding community, Revolution NYC holds its gatherings in local bars, music venues, coffee shops and a candy store. People from the community hear about the hope of the gospel in their own backyard. On a broader scale, the popular Revolution NYC podcast at iTunes garners greater interest and momentum.

In Irish Gaeilge the word *samhlaigh* means to imagine or to visualize. Revolution NYC has a *samhlaigh* ministry; its creative incitement is rooted firmly in the center of the world it hopes to reach; its art doesn't hide from uncomfortable realities but points the way clearly to freedom. Creative inciters likewise have a ministry of *samhlaigh*: we are compelled by the gospel to free those who have disqualified themselves from the possibility of God's grace. From the center of our culture we can imagine, engage and reawaken a gospel freedom to live life; we can dismantle the walls that have been erected around the kingdom of God once and for all.

FOR REFLECTION AND DISCUSSION

1. As an artist or creative inciter, what is the conviction of your life that causes you to live radically?

2. How do you use your art to shape your reality? To shape your circle of influence?

3. What are the "right questions" your art is asking? What questions *should* your art be asking?

Part Three

ACTIVISM

For any given human being in a particular cultural environment, all it takes to change their world—to change the horizons of possibility and impossibility for them—is to change the culture right around them.

Andy Crouch, *Culture Making*

7

COLOR ME HUMAN

Silence is the real crime
against humanity.

NADEZHDA MANDELSTAM,
Hope Against Hope

As we have seen, creative incitement ultimately comes down to taking part in righting the wrongs of our world. Dealing compassionately with those trapped by injustice and disrespect is *the* primary value of those who recognize we are made in the image of the almighty Creator.

Someone has said that Jesus came to afflict the comfortable and comfort the afflicted. I think this is a pretty good standard to hold. Whether it's people of a different age, gender, race, social or marital status, or sexual orientation, discrimination and inequity are inherently anti-Christian.

Therefore, part of our work must be helping others see injustice and inequality in our communities.

Window Dressing

An acrylic painting highly textured with subtle images in the background of different clothes hanging on laundry lines between buildings. This painting reflects the gritty, working-class, urban feel that reminds me of the flats on the north side of the River Liffey, Dublin, Ireland, near where I once lived and worked in full-time ministry. (Courtesy of DankoArtStudio.com)

WHEN I BECAME AN ACTIVIST

While working and living overseas, I witnessed prejudices and tension reminiscent of the American South during the civil rights movement. What America struggled with then, other countries and cultures were experiencing only a matter of years ago. In disadvantaged city areas with trash and broken glass littering the streets, and burned-out cars smoldering next to streetlights, I worked with children who had little hope or prospect of breaking free from the cycle of poverty they and their single-parent families were trapped in.

I recall in disturbing detail a young Nigerian immigrant boy named Abejedi walking in a group of several other children, with myself and two summer interns from the community center, to the nearby football pitch for a game of "footy." As we passed through the Tallaght housing estate, a lower-income suburb of Dublin, Abejedi was suddenly circled by a group of eight-year-old girls in school uniforms. Like a pack of ravenous wolves snarling and snapping, these young girls hurled insults and racial slurs, calling him a dog and shouting at the top of their voices for him to go home.

It was painfully apparent this wasn't the first time Abe had experienced this form of abuse. Neighbors peered from windows and front doors, and others poured out onto the street from their working-class row homes. But they came only to watch, not to come to his defense. One intern distracted the young girls as I and the other intern grabbed Abe and sped down the street to safety, our own hearts violently pounding in our ears.

I also remember the shocking brutality imposed on a nineteen-year-old Northern Irish lad, nailed to a fence in the shape of a crucifix because he was wearing a historically Catholic football team jersey. He had mistakenly crossed over into the edge of a Protestant housing estate, only to learn firsthand how cruel and vile people can be to one another.

Prejudice and poverty know no boundaries; they do not respect God, man or beast. But for people of faith there can be no race beyond human. Those who feel entitled to an identity beyond this have never faced the horrors of people attempting to strip them of their humanity. After peering into the pain-stricken eyes of those trapped in the cycles of poverty, sexual exploitation and prejudice, my heart and mind could not escape their unspoken pleas: *"Color me human."*

How we respond to our fellow humans reveals our own true colors, which lie beneath the surface of our skin. As the Bible appropriately puts it,

> As water reflects the face,
>   so one's life reflects the heart. (Proverbs 27:19)

Each of us has unthinkable capacities in us. We see it in our world almost every day. Dehumanizing others is a learned behavior, passed from one generation to the next. Those girls who terrorized Abe, those Protestants who terrorized that young Northern Irish man—they were merely reflecting what had been modeled. Our inhumanity toward others is nothing new under the sun. When I went to Ireland, I had a vision of engaging non-Christians with art. I didn't have much more than that. But in time, a community grew that was engaging people on a real level through our shared goal of using art to connect and slowly right the injustice of disconnection and disaffection.

Martin Luther King Jr. wrote from a Birmingham jail demonstrating the impulse of a creative inciter:

I am in Birmingham because injustice is here. . . .

Injustice anywhere is a threat to justice everywhere. We are caught in an inescapable network of mutuality, tied in a single garment of destiny. Whatever affects one directly, affects all indirectly.[1]

We know our relationship with God affects our relationship with one another, which affects our influence on a skeptical, watching world.

So what is our relationship with one another meant to look like?

PERSONAL ACTIVISM

The greatest commandment Jesus gave is, "Love the Lord your God with all your heart and with all your soul and with all your mind and with all your strength." But he didn't stop there. "The second is this: 'Love your neighbor as yourself.' There is no greater commandment than these" (Mark 12:30-31). Jesus said, "Whatever you did for one of the least of these brothers and sisters of mine, you did for me" (Matthew 25:40). Loving others with Jesus' sincere love *is* loving God.

Loving our neighbors requires us to be creative. Helping others can involve caring for their physical needs in various ways. But it also requires engaging with their humanity, affirming them and lifting their spirits with hope in creative, demonstrable ways. When we as artists have linked the pain of our own back stories and seen the remaking of our lives into something beautiful, we can share this breath of life with others and bring deep sighs of satisfaction to a suffering soul.

The Russian writer and philosopher Fyodor Dostoevsky said, "To love someone means to see him as God intended him." To love as creative inciters is to see the world through the lenses of grace, mercy and love—to not see people as they are but as they could be. This kind of creative love allows for the incitement that transforms societies and cultures, that tears down walls of division.

Martin Luther King Jr. observed,

> Cowardice asks the question, is it safe? Expediency asks the question, is it politic? Vanity asks the question, is it popular? But conscience asks the question, is it right? And there comes a time when one must take a position that is neither safe, nor politic, nor popular, but he must do it because conscience tells him it is right.[2]

Creative inciters regularly and consciously reject cowardice, expediency and vanity when they inevitably present themselves; creative inciters commit themselves from the outset to listening to conscience first and last.

When we listen to our conscience instead of vanity, expediency and cowardice, not only is our art affected but our context, since context is part of the essence of art. When we only surround ourselves with people who are pleasant, clean and respectable to the eyes, we lose sight of the face of the poor and oppressed, and disregard the pain and suffering around us. Likewise, if we avoid those that hold opposing worldviews, we forget that they exist alongside us, that in this lost and dying world are people who have no idea how much their Creator actually loves them.

Cowardice, expediency and vanity plague us, softly whispering in our ears, "Is it safe, is it politic, is it popular?" But conscience rightfully retorts, "Is it right?" Extending love in tangible ways—becoming the hands and feet of God—is an act of creation that is incompatible with cowardice, expediency and vanity, but we are assured in the midst of it that it is right. The evidence of our faith contains true power and love, for we not only see through the lenses of grace, mercy and love; we live through it.

We assume a lot in life. Many of us go about our business thinking most of the world lives at a standard much like that of our own. Our unspoken assumption is that most people have clean water, electricity and the amenities we take for granted. In reality most of the world sleeps whole households in one room; more than 900 million people go hungry every day. With the increase of natural disasters, drought and war, that number continues to inch closer and closer to one billion.

Being open to life is often difficult, but withdrawing from it, whether intentionally or not, brings its own perils. Life would be far easier if we didn't need to have a heart, if we could simply delude ourselves into a life of safety, popularity and expediency. But caring is our instinct and our calling; being people of faith guarantees us nothing but a responsibility to the poor and marginalized among us.

A DEAFENING SILENCE

In her memoirs *Hope Against Hope* and *Hope Abandoned,* the Russian-born writer and educator Nadezhda (*Nah-DEZH-dah,* which means "hope") Mandelstam criticized the cultural and moral deterioration of the Soviet Union under the repressive regime of Joseph Stalin. Prior to her own literary work, both Nadezhda and her husband, Osip, were exiled from the Ukraine to the federal district of Cherdyn, Perm Krai, Russia. They were forbidden to enter the largest cities in the Soviet Union, which were the cultural and artistic centers, due to Osip's satirical poem "Stalin Epigram."

This scathing literary indictment of Joseph Stalin and his directorate was largely responsible for Osip's arrest and imprisonment. After her husband's death at a transit camp to a gulag in Siberia, Nadezhda led a nomadic life; she frequently changed residences and worked temporary jobs in order to avoid arrest and further persecution. After twenty years in an internal exile, upon Stalin's death she was allowed by the Khrushchev government to return to Moscow, where she completed her studies in linguistics and soon became a published author. "Silence," she wrote, "is the real crime against humanity."[3] By doing nothing when we have the means, we allow God's love to pass from any given moment.

Solomon wrote in Ecclesiastes about how momentary our lives are in the light of eternity:

Generations come and generations go. . . .
The sun rises and the sun sets,
    and hurries back to where it rises. (Ecclesiastes 1:4-5)

Simply put, we're here today, gone tomorrow. Isaiah came to a similar conclusion:

All people are like grass,
    and all their faithfulness is like the flowers of the field;
the grass withers and the flowers fall. (Isaiah 40:6-7)

Such insight into the human condition can make us feel hopeless and cause us to abdicate our responsibility to the moments God has given us. Yet the apostle Paul provides us with a biblical wake-up call:

Everything exposed by the light becomes visible. . . . This is why it is said:

"Wake up, sleeper,
 rise from the dead,
 and Christ will shine on you." (Ephesians 5:13-14)

The world doesn't need us to talk more, to share more or to create more awareness, because awareness in and of itself does not incite or equate to actual activism. The world needs us to shine, which happens when we "live as children of light (for the fruit of the light consists in all goodness, righteousness and truth)" (Ephesians 5:8-9).

Rather than writing a little bit of history by living out the gospel with intention and an outward focus, we too often settle for the seductive call to success. Instead, Solomon advises, we should make the most of our moments:

Remember [your Creator]—before the silver cord is severed,
 and the golden bowl is broken;
before the pitcher is shattered at the spring,
 and the wheel broken at the well,
and the dust returns to the ground it came from,
 and the spirit returns to God who gave it. (Ecclesiastes
 12:6-7)

One summer I traveled from Dublin to Bantry, County Cork, to lead a three-day songwriting workshop. We studied song structure, arrangement, lyrics and more; then we applied what we learned in practical ways. It was a safe place for the exchange of ideas with musicians and songwriters from different cultures and backgrounds in the United States, Northern Ireland and the Republic of Ireland. The first day everyone got to know one another over cups of tea and biscuits. We shared stories, laughter and original songs with the group. I then grouped everyone in pairs and asked them to write one original composition, which would be presented to our creative group the last day of the workshop. It was inspiring to see the creative spirit unleashed in people; their imaginations not only widened but in some cases soared.

After a brief recap of the workshop and what seemed to conclude our time together, I walked toward the door to exit, hesitated momentarily, then turned and announced that I would see everyone at ten that night at a local public house down the road for an open songwriter night. Some chuckled and snickered, others laughed it off, thinking I was messing with them.

"No, really," I assured them. "I spoke with the pub manager, and you're on at 10 p.m. The locals from the town will be attending. I expect to see each of you there." An awkward uneasiness rose and silence entered the room as I exited to the street and an unusually beautiful Irish summer day.

The time for the gig arrived, as did each person who had attended the songwriting workshop. You could feel the nervous apprehension as they tuned, retuned and retuned guitar strings, rat-a-tat-tatted a small weathered drum kit and nervously thumped the bodhrán, an Irish drum. After a hearty Irish welcome and brief introduction came an awkward pause. No volunteers to kick off the session were to be found. The audience cleared their throats, and I gathered myself, stepped to the microphone and shared two original songs and the inspiration behind their stories.

After that it was like watching dominoes fall one by one. My workshop colleagues played their songs, and more and more people gathered to listen. Even some of the local musicians joined in for a jam session. It became a standing-room-only event.

Interestingly enough, as the night progressed, so did the interactions—from informal chitchat to more in-depth conversations. It was marvelous to see the commonality of music allowing us to move beyond our protectiveness and into each other's lives without agenda or goals. We had pursued the freedom to create dangerously, risked opening up with strangers, and trusted God would use that as he saw fit.

And what a night it was.

I have found over and over again, when we reach out to engage with a hurting world, the world *wants* us to succeed in all we do. Open up and share your art and you may just find the "spirit return[ing] to God who gave it."

FOR REFLECTION AND DISCUSSION

1. How do you respond to the idea that "silence is the great crime against humanity"? What are some of the ways you have remained silent?

2. What examples of prejudice and self-absorption do you see in the world?

3. What are some ways you can exercise faith and engage with a hurting world without an agenda or goals?

8

THE GOD OF
ORDINARY PEOPLE

The Master of Life's been good to me.
He has given me strength to face past illnesses,
and victory in the face of defeat. He has given me life
and joy where others saw oblivion. He has given
new purpose to live for, new services to render
and old wounds to heal. Life and
love go on, let the music play.

JOHNNY CASH,
quoted in *The Man Comes Around*

Let me set the record straight. I'm not a theologian, and as I said in a prior chapter, I'm certainly not a model Christian. In fact, I'm more of a model sinner—desperately in need of God's grace on a moment-by-moment basis. And yes, I'm okay with this.

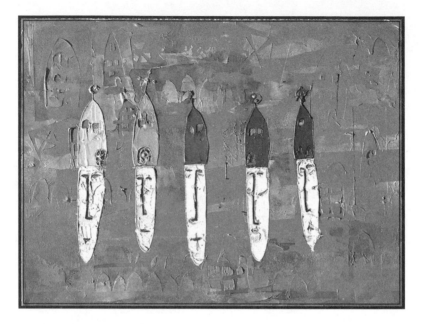

So Many Choices, So Little Time

Rich, vibrant acrylic colors and a deep, textured background add more than a hint of movement and energy to this piece of art. I selected the title *So Many Choices, So Little Time* because life offers so much to see and experience, but there's simply not enough time to do it all. Ultimately, we just have to make choices and live life the best we can. (Courtesy of DankoArtStudio.com)

We seem to have concluded that God chooses to only use spiritual giants—the highly gifted, multitalented, faith-filled people of this world, and not spiritual pygmies like me and perhaps you. But frankly, nothing could be further from the truth. In fact, God has a well-documented history of working through the broken vessels of this world, "the scalawags and ragamuffins" as Brennan Manning put it.

ENGAGING, THEN INFLUENCING

During my time in Dublin, I was involved in a progressive social initiative program. We had a small band of Irish and American visual artists, musicians and creatives. We invited nonbelievers to join and create art collectively, asking real-life questions. Despite our imperfections God used us to influence others and become creative inciters. Our community of artisans held exhibits in neutral venues (not churches), did music performances on the streets of Dublin and in other city centers, in pubs, and art festivals—engaging with people from different walks of life and at varying points in their life journeys.

In collaboration with like-minded creatives, I developed and introduced music business training programs in songwriting, record production, performance, marketing and promotion, and live events. We also launched film and multimedia courses, visual art and theater production classes, all designed to arm young people in a disadvantaged section of Dublin with work and life skills to provide opportunity to break through the cycles of poverty and drugs.

One particular instance impressed on me how crucial my role was to engage and influence these young men and women's lives. When it was time for tea, a trolley cart rolled in with hot kettles of water and mounds of scones and muffins. It was like the air escaped the room. All eyes followed the cart as its wheels squeaked and wobbled. Soon, the break was announced and everyone made a beeline for the trolley cart. It didn't stand a chance. These children and teens from Ballyfermot stuffed their coat pockets full. It was their one opportunity to have enough food to eat in the coming days—or in a few cases, an entire week.

I held my breath to finish teaching the class and I dismissed the students. Several stayed behind to talk, and as we parted ways, I shook their hands, thanking each of them for attending; I would hope to see them next week. When I was alone in the cold, damp classroom, I glanced down and my hand was black with soot and grime. It was from the kids' hands. Tears welled up as I fought to hold back the flood. I made my way to the "gents room" to wash, choking back the tears as I watched the swirling dirty water in the basin. The gravity of engaging those precious souls and then working to *influence* their lives struck me head-on with a force I will never forget.

These were the very people I knew God had brought me to serve, for his reasons and for my own sake. And I couldn't have been more grateful for them.

For his good reasons God has always preferred to use questionable characters of little social standing, the ill-tempered, deniers of the faith, liars, adulterers, prostitutes, murderers and scandalous riffraff to convey the good news and accomplish his good purposes. For just one example, even after committing adultery, which led to murder, David was called by no less than God "a man after his own heart." Similarly Paul reminds us,

> Take a good look, friends, at who you were when you got called into this life. I don't see many of "the brightest and the best" among you, not many influential, not many from high-society families. Isn't it obvious that God deliberately chose men and women that the culture overlooks and exploits and abuses, chose these "nobodies" to expose the hollow pretensions of the "somebodies"? (1 Corinthians 1:26-28 *The Message*)

THE GOOD COMPANY OF QUESTIONABLE CHARACTERS

We find it far more pleasant to be known and seen for our strengths, not for our flaws or weaknesses. But in his infinite wisdom God chooses to use ordinary people, imperfect ambassadors of the gospel, to reach out in faith to people just like us. In doing so we are in the good company of questionable characters and surrounded by a great cloud of witnesses. That's how this extraordinary God is revealed and encountered in the peaks and valleys of everyday circumstances and the ordinariness of life.

Who should we glean, and not glean, from? If we take this endeavor of creative incitement seriously, we'll need to carefully consider who we share our deepest selves with. Opening up to encourage others is an important practice to employ, but trust is built over time, and the benefits of long friendships are undeniable for the support and encouragement they offer.

Bottom line, creativity is an expensive resource. Many artists find it necessary to recharge within their few closest relationships. It pays to consider who your closest, like-minded artist inciters are—there will be times when you need them. Identifying and cultivating the relationships that build your personal community will reap benefits far beyond what you could manage on your own.

Before Jesus chose his closest helpers, he prayed. I imagine he prayed for people with many diverse qualities—inspiring, humble, talented, giving. But one thing I feel certain he prayed they'd all have: a deep love and longing for God. He could use most anyone really, but finding those who would truly love God, who'd want to serve him and be his flashlights in the dark world, Jesus knew this was all-important.

When you pray for fellow inciters, ask God to reveal those he's been longing to connect us with for their deep need of him.

Then seek them out! There are always deeply committed people looking for this vision and eager to discuss and define their larger ministry of creative incitement through their art.

One great way to do this is through getting involved in Christian parachurch (independent cross-denominational) groups and gatherings. Ben Arment is the founder of STORY Conference, currently held each year in downtown Chicago. To encourage creative inciters from abandoning their creative calling, Ben envisioned a gathering of people producing creative and redemptive works of art in the most unlikely, unexpected places and through varied mediums. This collection of creatives has come to understand the power of turning experiences into story and seeing those stories enriched, expressed in diversified forms, which ultimately helps us to better understand and make sense of our lives in a tumultuous world. It brings not *what if* but the more generative *why not* question, delivering the art of revolutionary rabble-rousers that encourages us to share our stories, repair what's fragmented in us, and observe how the gospel can be found in the arts again.

THE POWER OF PERSONAL SACRIFICE

In the early 1920s, during the Russian Civil War, the Bolshevik Red Army fought alongside leftist pro-revolutionary groups against allied but loosely organized anti-Bolshevik forces, known as the White Army. A small village fell to the Red Army, and a woman and her two small children found themselves in grave danger, since her husband had been fighting for the White Army. She and her children hid for some time in an abandoned house, looking for the opportunity to escape.

Early one evening a young woman knocked at the door. With her children huddled beside her, the woman cracked the door open slightly so they would remain in the shadows. The young woman told the older woman that she and her children had been discovered; they were to be detained and shot that night. The young woman implored her to take her children and escape immediately. The mother looked down at her children and expressed her despair. "How could I?" she sighed, feeling hopeless.

At that point the young woman became a bearer of the gospel. "I will stay behind and call myself by your name when they come for you."

The mother responded, "But you will be shot."

"Yes, that is true—but I have no children," replied the young neighbor. And so, she remained behind in the damp, cold, abandoned home with the gloom and darkness of night wrapping itself around her as she waited for her impending death.

Like Christ in the Garden of Gethsemane, this young woman probably hoped that this cup could pass her by. She may have wondered what would become of the mother and her children, and prayed that her sacrifice not be in vain, but her only answer was the words of Christ in the Gospel of John: "Greater love has no one than this: to lay down one's life for one's friends" (John 15:13). The young woman was seized, and as the crack of gunfire echoed through the small village that night, she died. The mother and children escaped; they lived because another died in their place.

What would our response be to Jesus' question to Peter: "Do you love me?" (John 21:17)? Our only appropriate and relinquishing response may well be worship—the kind of worship that is lived out and flows from our lives into the lives of others.

That young woman who gave her life for her neighbor was worshiping as she did it. Our ultimate act of worship is our expression of the deep, abiding, sacrificial love shown by a Father that tenderly cares for and loves his children. Our opportunity as creative inciters is to worship by re-creating Christ's ministry of selflessness, self-sacrifice and obedience to the will and purposes of God. Such worship illustrates the freedom found in Christ and freely given to those who follow him.

HOT WHISKEY TO FEED HIS SHEEP

After walking for almost two kilometers in gale-force winds and lashing rain toward the small northwest Irish village of Glencolumbkille, County Donegal, a friend and I finally arrived at a remote local pub. We settled in front of an open hearth filled with burning bricks of smoking peat to dry out our drenched clothes and souls. As we shivered and sipped our mugs of hot whiskey, steaming with scents of lemon and clove, my friend came out with it: "Sometimes I'm tempted to ask God why he can allow all the suffering and injustice in the world when he could certainly do something about it."

I paused momentarily, and in between cold shivers and sips I responded, "Why don't you ask him?"

As only an Irishman can, he quickly fired back, "I would, but I'm afraid he'd ask me the same question."

Whether my friend was "borrowing like an artist" with that line or not, it really isn't enough for us to be informed or to be concerned in the moment about such things. As the extraordinary God of ordinary people once said to Peter, if we love God, we're called to feed his sheep.

God uses people like you and me to use the currencies of our time, talent and resources to feed the hungry, clothe the poor, heal the sick and share the good news. God recognizes remarkable potential and purpose where we may see nothing of the kind. The beauty of the Christian faith is that it is offered to everyone, even as it demands that we do whatever we can, whenever we can, to care for those in need.

THE IMMEASURABLE DISTANCE

Like God, the world is watching what we do—and noting what we choose not to do. People outside the faith are conscious of the immeasurable distance between what they read in Scripture and what the church actually practices. But we can't allow that scrutiny to petrify us; in fact we must push beyond it to achieve real connection with those outside the faith. As the Dutch-born Catholic priest and writer Henri Nouwen wrote,

> Traveling is joyful when we travel with the eyes and ears of those who love us, who want to see our slides and hear our stories. This is what life is about. It is being sent on a trip by a loving God, who is waiting at home for our return and is eager to watch the slides we took and hear about the friends we made. When we travel with the eyes and ears of the God who sent us, we will see wonderful sights, hear wonderful sounds, meet wonderful people . . . and be happy to return home.[1]

If you're fully immersed in it, the gospel, much like art, comes out in life—whatever you do. It's the full immersion in what God is doing, wherever he takes you, whatever happens in life, that makes a life of creative incitement. In any community of believing creatives, you'll be tapped in.

So use your God-given creativity! And may God graciously allow each of us to reach out across the immeasurable distance in our own time of need and faithfully practice the *art* of helping others—in whatever ways he provides.

This indeed is what living is all about.

FOR REFLECTION AND DISCUSSION

1. What are some of the ways that you personally have seen ordinary people do extraordinary things?

2. Who are some of the people God brought to mind as you thought about your closest fellow inciters?

3. What are some of the ways you can defy the norm or status quo of society and create a legacy that will outlive you for generations to come?

9

COME DIE WITH US

Vision without action is merely a dream.
Action without vision just passes the time.
Vision with action can change the world.

JOEL BARKER,
The Star Thrower Story

My father is an amazing person. Now in his nineties, he has an unyielding energy and enthusiasm to live life to its fullest. Long before retiring from the military as a decorated United States Army Ranger and Master Paratrooper, he enrolled in evening university courses, studying for more than ten years in order to receive his bachelor's degree. He went on to teach elementary school children, became a school principal, received his master's degree in education and then retired from that second career. For more than twenty years now, he's worked a third vocation at a vineyard, eventually being recognized as a master pruner. That task requires him to nurture, prune, cut and shape the cordon (the arms of the

Home Is Where You Are

The phrase "Home Is Where You Are" came to me after living in my '96 Jeep for a brief time. This painting resembles my life as well as that of many others. The colorful, multi-layered, textured house in a sense personifies who we are beneath our neatly layered facades. We travel on disjointed floor levels barely held together, rolling down a slanted street on worn wheels—very much like the circumstances of everyday life we encounter. The Cyrillic letters are Russian for "home." (Courtesy of DankoArtStudio.com) grapevine), which ultimately determines the grape clusters that will reach their full potential to be harvested for production. This necessitates that he have a vision and passion for what he does.

In everything he has been tasked with, my father has always faithfully produced results. It's one of the many attributes that I profoundly respect him for. In this respect, his work ethic always reminds me of the parable of the talents.

Matthew's account of this parable (see Matthew 25) goes something like this:

- Employer prepared for an extensive leave of absence from work due to travel.

- Employer gathered his employees and entrusted his finances and property to them, including clear expectations of success.

- Employer returned from his extensive travel, gathered his long-time employees to receive a report as to how they invested and cared for what was entrusted to them.

- Employee One invested wisely and made a killing, a 100 percent gain.

- Employee Two achieved a 50 percent increase.

- Employer was so pleased that he rewarded them with even greater responsibilities and recognition.

- Employee Three decided to set aside what had been entrusted to him. In so doing he also laid aside the charge that came with it—the expectations of success that the employer had clearly detailed. This employee achieved nothing beyond what he started with; he didn't even open a savings account to earn interest on the investment.

- Employer was less than pleased with this lack of drive and initiative; he took away what had been assigned to the third employee and pulled the plug on his career.

The primary point of this parable is, of course, not about money management. It is about living the Christian life. As followers of Christ we have been called to more than playing it safe; the Christian life involves choosing a path that engages reality and produces results.

Like a vineyard caretaker entrusted with much responsibility, creative inciters start with something given to us; we are judged by how we prune and shape what we're given, how we transform our creative ideas into real action.

FINDING WHAT REMAINS

Every creative enterprise begins with taking stock of what you have. Just as a sailboat and its crew should never take to sea without indispensable items like trustworthy sails, a stalwart anchor and a charted course, your successful vocation as a creative inciter may begin with your own personal manifesto—the stock you take of what you have within you. It took me far too long to acknowledge the importance of developing such a manifesto—a mission statement for myself that articulates particular ideals and aspirations—committing myself every day to living it out to the best of my ability.

When I lived in my Jeep—an 8' x 5' living space littered with handwritten notes, two small black suitcases stuffed with all the clothing I had, three pairs of well-used shoes, one frayed striped blanket, a pillow and a spare tire—I tried my best to hold things together on my own. Wrestling under the stress, shame and heart-wrenching ending of a long-term relationship, the long suffering and eventual loss of my mother, huge financial strain, and various other issues made for the perfect storm as my thin walls slowly closed in on me. From my Jeep I could see the businesses and shops open and close, and the image of Atlas with the world on his shoulders was all too real to me, and it felt as if my knees would buckle any moment, collapsing and crushing me.

Ignoring the imbalance of life led me to self-condemnation. I felt defeated; I was a catastrophic disaster even though deep down I knew better. But no matter what I tried to do, I couldn't push the dark clouds away. The suffocating weight of self-doubt set me on a drunken spin of navel-gazing and anger as I questioned God. "Where are you?" I screamed into the silence.

Yet I found, in time, he'd never left. Like drawing the untapped water from a deeper well in a drought-stricken desert, he knew this plunging experience was exactly what I needed to be able to draw deeper from him. That isolation and deeply painful journey was what it took to pierce the veil and force me to suddenly see my own manifesto, the need for it and my real need to act on it. And as A. W. Tozer says in *The Pursuit of God*, "Ransomed men need no longer pause in fear to enter the Holy of Holies. God wills that we should push on into His Presence and live our whole life there. This is to be known to us in conscious experience."[1]

I learned during that time that home is always where you are. We roll down slanted streets on frayed tires, barely held together, shifting and lurching as we hit the occasional life lesson pothole. My time living out of my car brought a plethora of positive commitments: it allowed me to see that there is no time like the present to start living the life I imagined; it helped me not to be a slave to work—not to let a job define and consume me. And it also taught me to determine what I wanted to do in life; it helped me to develop a plan and pursue it with fervor.

My personal manifesto includes the idea that worship should never exist merely to serve itself; the byproduct of that idea is that my God-given creativity and creative incitement should help to inspire, strengthen and build the church. That may entail instigating constructive action and inciting risk through visual art, books or other creative projects. Another natural outcome is that I help redefine expressions of worship in people's imagination. That's how I now endeavor to live this aspect of my life and work at my art.

A second fundamental tenet of my manifesto is that I have determined not to be drawn into any needless drama. I've lived through enough abuse. I came to this conviction as a result of painful past relationships, including being used by those I believe were sincerely well-meaning, but getting "brothered" to death by those with nothing more to offer than overworked clichés—"God is in control"—which essentially proved he was actively choosing to do nothing. Easy answers get applied to times of immediate crisis but are effectively forgotten during times of relative calm.

How do you develop your own personal manifesto? I'm not going to claim to be an authority on the subject, but what worked for me was to be honest enough with myself to write statements about who I am at the deepest level. This helped me to construct a basic foundation to establish my core ideals, beliefs and aspirations, to identify a theme that cuts through all the noise and clutter and reflects my view of the world.

While this kind of self-assessment can be intimidating, it can lead to a plan that is realistic and energizing; it can incite your own vocation of creative incitement.

EXACTLY WHAT WE DON'T NEED

Remember, God doesn't necessarily need more theologians, pastors, seminary graduates or full-time Christian workers. God wants everyday people like you and me who the average person grinding through daily life can relate to. This insight makes me fall back into my chair far more differently now than ever before. I no longer shift uncomfortably or sigh in deep anxiety; instead I marvel at my always-unfolding journey. I sporadically stumble as I move forward, but I gather myself more easily, knowing that God goes before me and is with me, and I keep moving through a world that I've come to recognize as full of mystery, truth and wonder.

Along the way I have amazing conversations that reveal the need for creative inciters to push regularly beyond the church. Worship is something that is always in constant, fluid, forward motion. It may not look like the status quo; it may be unacceptable to the forces of traditionalism and defenders of the old order. It may have a sacrificial quality to it, like birth pains giving way to creative incitement heralding the kingdom of God.

Whatever your specific expression, in art or through your keen awareness of real life, or activist initiatives, will you finally decide to claim your birthright as one made in the image of the Creator? Will you join your own creative calling to that of your other creative inciters and risk takers? The extraordinary God of ordinary people is affectionately murmuring in the wind, "Come die with us." It's a sacred invitation, a divine provocation for us to die to ourselves each day, to embrace a more expansive life, one not limited to our own.

But beware, this life may entail walking away from the accolades and the prospects of worldly success. It may not look like what you expect right now.

However, there is an even greater kingdom our souls gravitate toward, and we will find it in the fullness of time.

FOR REFLECTION AND DISCUSSION

1. What is your personal manifesto? Don't have one? What are you waiting for? Start now.

2. What expressions of worship are you eager to explore in your life now? Painting? Music? Writing? Planting a garden? Starting a quiet revolution in your neighborhood?

3. Will you pray for God's insight in putting your God-given desire for creative incitement to work? And then when he responds, will you *do* it?

Appendix

SOME WAYS TO DIE WITH US

There are many organizations and people doing great things for those in need. You could apply your own creative gifts to support and be involved with any of them, not to mention your local church. There are also organizations that look good on the surface but whose work is not truly transforming the world according to God's vision, and there are other perfectly good organizations that for any number of reasons would not align well with your personal manifesto. It's worth doing some research before you commit yourself.

Here is a short list of organizations to consider as starting points in your search to implement your manifesto and practice the art of helping others.

ART

STORY is an annual conference for the creative class in ministry. Held in Chicago, the goal of STORY is to fuel those who live to communicate the gospel through creative incitement. Presenters include some of the best creative practitioners in both ministry and the marketplace, from filmmakers and authors to actors and musicians, all helping people engage others in the most compelling and effective way. Find out more at storychicago.com.

International Arts Movement, a nonprofit organization founded by Makoto Fujimura, gathers artists and creative catalysts to wrestle with the deep questions of art, faith and humanity, in order to inspire the creative community to engage the culture that is and create the world that ought to be. IAM organizes programming that provides artists of all disciplines opportunities to rehumanize the world around them through the creative arts. Find out more at internationalartsmovement.org.

TheArtofHelpingOthers.com is the website for this book and is intended as a constructive call to action among artists, musicians, writers, creatives and churches through art, awareness and activism.

AWARENESS

Sevenly is an organization with a mission to be the world's most effective cause-activation platform, leading a generation toward intentional generosity and love for others. Sevenly reviews charitable humanitarian causes each week, and for every T-shirt purchased, a designated dollar amount is contributed to that cause. Learn more at sevenly.org.

Kiva is a nonprofit organization with a mission to connect people through lending to alleviate poverty. Leveraging the Internet and a worldwide network of microfinance institutions, Kiva lets individuals lend as little as $25 to help create opportunity around the world. Find out more at kiva.org.

Christian Alliance for Orphans unites more than eighty respected Christian organizations and a national network of churches to help Christians understand God's call to care for orphans and to equip them for effective response far beyond a single program or met need. Find out more at christianalliancefororphans.org.

Trade as One uses fair trade to promote sustainable business with a mission to break the cycles of poverty and dependency in developing countries. They help the poor use their skills to work their way from poverty to transformed lives. Learn more at tradeasone.com.

ACTIVISM

International Justice Mission is a human rights agency that secures justice for victims of slavery, sexual exploitation and other forms of violent oppression. IJM lawyers, investigators and aftercare professionals work with local governments to ensure victim rescue, to prosecute perpetrators, and to strengthen the community and civic factors that promote functioning public justice systems. Find out more at ijm.org.

Oxfam is an international confederation of fifteen organizations working together in over ninety countries. With partners and allies around the world, they find lasting solutions to poverty and injustice. Oxfam works directly with communities and seeks to influence the powerful to ensure that poor people can improve their lives and livelihoods, and have a say in decisions that affect them. Learn more at oxfam.org.

Sojourners is a Christian organization whose mission is to articulate the biblical call to social justice, inspiring hope and building a movement to transform individuals, communities, the church and the world. Find out more at sojo.net.

ACKNOWLEDGMENTS

Don Pape, whose encouragement was instrumental in seeing that these words found their way to you.

Mick Silva, John Blaise and David Zimmerman for their expertise and superb editorial guidance.

Everyone at InterVarsity Press for their incredible support and for allowing me to ask more questions than provide answers.

Robert Brenner for his pastoral perseverance and ministerial nudges.

Also Nataliya Burdeynyuk, Bruno and Jennifer Pirecki, our best friend Skagit, Don Simpson, Brennan Manning, Francis and Lisa Chan, Dan Rich, Chris Curry, Jeff Moseley, Mark Adkison, Bruce Fitzhugh, Mike and Kim Kennedy, Amy and Brad Quicksall, Thom and Kate Hoyman, Mike Ruman, Wade Olinger of Connected Churches, Craig Thompson and the Disciple Design team, David Terry, Phillip Parker Photography, Luke Bolin and Shawn Gourley at Edison Creative, everyone at fastPXL.com, Daniel Bashta, Leslie Jordan and Dave Leonard of All Sons & Daughters, Ben Arment and all at the STORY Conference, Karen Stoller, Annette Brickbealer, Danko Art Studio, Jeane and Tyson Wynn at Wynn Wynn Media, Barry Higginbotham, Chris Estes, Shannon and Gary Walker, Sheila Crocker,

Jessica Chappell, "Wild Bill" Collier, Mike Morrell, Ryan Wood and everyone at Sevenly.org, JB and all those across the pond, John Paculabo, Café 615 on beloved Dauphin Street, Carpe Diem Coffee & Tea Co., Agia Sophia, Humble Pie Store on Elati, Ben Robinson, all my friends and family in the United States, Ukraine, Eire and the United Kingdom, Claus and Helen Mann, my brothers Dave and Russ and their families, the Ralstons for the use of their Rocky Mountain cabin, Meshu, who traveled part of this journey, and all those that could have lived up to what Oscar Wilde once said: "True friends stab you in the front." Plus anyone I've failed to thank because of a limited word count for acknowledgments.

NOTES

CHAPTER 2: CALLING ALL CREATIVE INCITERS

[1]Henry David Thoreau, *Walden*, ed. Raymond MacDonald Alden, Longmans' English Classics (New York: Longmans, Green and Company, 1910), p. 259.
[2]G. K. Chesterton, *The Ballad of the White Horse* (New York: John Lane, 1911), book II.
[3]Henry David Thoreau, *The Portable Thoreau*, ed. Carl Bode (New York: Penguin Books, 1982), pp. 342-43.
[4]Andy Crouch, *Culture Making* (Downers Grove, IL: InterVarsity Press, 2008), p. 97.

CHAPTER 3: FISHERS OF ZEN

[1]Oscar Wilde, *Lady Windermere's Fan* (Seattle: CreateSpace, 2012), p. 58.
[2]Brandi Carlile, "The Story," Warner/Chappell Music, 2007.
[3]Charlotte Elliott, "Just as I Am," 1835.

CHAPTER 4: WORSHIP AS A CREATIVE LIFESTYLE

[1]Ben Cantelon, "Writers: Ben Cantelon," *We Are Worship*, www.weare worship.com/us/writers/ben-cantelon.
[2]Martin Luther King Jr., "Letter from Birmingham Jail," April 16, 1963. See www.africa.upenn.edu/Articles_Gen/Letter_Birmingham.html.
[3]Rich Mullins, concert at Carpenter's Way Christian Church, Lufkin, TX, July 19, 1997. See http://en.wikipedia.org/wiki/Rich_Mullins.

CHAPTER 5: BEYOND PROPAGANDA AND BOXES

[1]Steve Turner, *Imagine* (Downers Grove, IL: InterVarsity Press, 2001), p. 23.
[2]See C. S. Lewis, "Bluspels and Flalansferes," *Selected Literary Essays* (Cambridge: Cambridge University Press, 1969), 265.
[3]Daniel Bashta, "Like a Lion," Integrity/Columbia, 2011.

[4]Paul Zollo, *Songwriters on Songwriting* (Cambridge, MA: Da Capo Press, 1991), p. 565.

[5]Leo Tolstoy, "Epilogue to the Kreutzer Sonata," trans. Leo Wiener, University of Minnesota, www1.umn.edu/lol-russ/hpgary/russ1905/epilogue%20 to%20kreutzer%20sonata.htm.

CHAPTER 6: THE FREEDOM TO CREATE DANGEROUSLY

[1]*Slagging*, akin to the English term for "taking the piss" out of someone, is an acquired Irish art form of mockery and only ever done in the most generous way possible.

[2]See John Ortberg, "Jesus as Praying: Taking Time Alone with God," *JesusCentral .com*, www.jesuscentral.com/ji/jesus-parables-teachings/jesus-example/jesus -praying.php.

[3]Bertolt Brecht, cited in Peter Leonard and Peter McLaren, eds., *Paulo Freire: A Critical Encounter* (New York: Routledge, 1992), p. 80.

[4]Martin Luther King Jr., *Strength to Love*, gift ed. (Minneapolis: Fortress Press, 2010), pp. 1-2.

CHAPTER 7: COLOR ME HUMAN

[1]Martin Luther King Jr., "Letter from Birmingham Jail," April 16, 1963. See www.africa.upenn.edu/Articles_Gen/Letter_Birmingham.html.

[2]Martin Luther King Jr., "A Proper Sense of Priorities," February 6, 1968, Washington, DC. See *Speeches and Sounds*, www.aavw.org/special_features /speeches_speech_king04.html.

[3]Nadezhda Mandelstam, *Hope Against Hope* (New York: Modern Library 1999), p. 43.

CHAPTER 8: THE GOD OF ORDINARY PEOPLE

[1]Henri J. M. Nouwen, *Bread for the Journey* (San Francisco: HarperOne, 2006), p. 100.

CHAPTER 9: COME DIE WITH US

[1]A. W. Tozer, *The Pursuit of God* (Radford, VA: Wilder Publications, 2008), p. 27.